P9-CEP-674

Motorbooks International Illustrated Buyer's Guide Series

Illustrated

FORD & FORDSON
TRACTOR
BUYER'S ★ GUIDE™

109070

Robert N. Pripps

ILLINOIS PRAIRIE DISTRICT LIBRARY

ILLINOIS PRAIRIE DPL

Motorbooks International
Publishers & Wholesalers ®

First published in 1994 by Motorbooks International Publishers & Wholesalers, PO Box 2, 729 Prospect Avenue, Osceola, WI 54020 USA

© Robert N. Pripps, 1994

All rights reserved. With the exception of quoting brief passages for the purpose of review no part of this publication may be reproduced without prior written permission from the Publisher

Motorbooks International is a certified trademark, registered with the United States Patent Office

The information in this book is true and complete to the best of our knowledge. All recommendations are made without any guarantee on the part of the author or Publisher, who also disclaim any liability incurred in connection with the use of this data or specific details

We recognize that some words, model names and designations, for example, mentioned herein are the property of the trademark holder. We use them for identification purposes only. This is not an official publication

Motorbooks International books are also available at discounts in bulk quantity for industrial or sales-promotional use. For details write to Special Sales Manager at the Publisher's address

Library of Congress Cataloging-in-Publication Data Available

ISBN 0-87938-890-0

On the front cover: The classic Ford 8N is especially popular with Ford collectors. It represents the ultimate in the art deco-styled N Series, especially the 1952 model (its last version) shown here. This beautiful 8N was restored and is owned by Dwight Emstrom, Galesburg, Illinois.

On the back cover: A 1963 Ford Jubilee driven by owner Mike Farrell; a 1942 Fordson N Standard photographed in Great Britain; and Dr. Jack Garner on his Ford 2000 Super Dexta.

Printed and bound in the United States of America

629.225 PRI
c. 1

Contents

Acknowledgments

I wish to thank the following helpful people and companies:

Palmer Fossum and Dwight Emstrom, two world-class Ford tractor collectors. Besides providing their many tractors to photograph, they provided me with many data details.

Marlo Remme, a Fordson expert who helped me with many of the details associated with those tractors.

Jack Heald, for providing me with a copy of his "The Real Fordson Story," published in *Gas Engines* magazine. This five-part article, co-authored by Thomas G. Brent, ran between July 1985 and November 1988. Anyone interested in all the details of the development of the Fordson should get this series.

Harold Brock, the design team leader at Ford during the development of the 9N and subsequent tractors, who provided many insights into the origins of the design. Brock personally knew Henry Ford, Charles Sorensen, and Harry Ferguson and his team.

Gerard Rinaldi, publisher of the *9N-2N-8N Newsletter*. By going over back issues of this newsletter, I was able to find out just about everything there is to know about these great tractors.

Jim Polacek of Polacek Implement, my Wisconsin Ford-New Holland dealer, for advice on old tractor collecting.

Randy Woker and Chris Shipman of Rock-Ford Tractor Sales and Service, Pecatonica, Illinois, my Illinois Ford tractor dealer and supplier of information and data for this book.

Artistic Photo Lab, Rockford, Illinois, for special attention to detail in developing my photos.

Michael Dregni, Motorbooks International's Editor in Chief, and his staff, and Michael Dapper, Editor, for pulling all this material together and making it look good.

Introduction

This book portrays in word and picture the first fifty years of Ford-built tractors. From 1917-1967, tractors by Ford had a profound impact on the agricultural industry of the world. For some reason, probably having to do with the number of them built, Fords and Fordsons have not enjoyed the same antique allure afforded contemporaries, especially the John Deere. Recently, however, things are beginning to change and Ford/Fordson collecting is catching on. My purpose in writing this book is to encourage and assist the potential collector, and to assure those already collecting of the historic value of their tractors.

Following a brief general history, the book is broken down into chapters on the Fordson, the Ford-Ferguson, post-war Fordsons, pre-1962 Fords, and post-1962 Fords. There is a description of each model and some comments on its collectibility. There is also a star rating assigned (see below), like those used in other Motorbooks International Illustrated Buyer's Guides. Chapter 9 describes how to buy and keep a collector tractor. An appendix lists some recommended reading material and parts sources.

Star Rating System

A star rating system is becoming standard among antique collectors to indicate at a glance the investment potential of a given vehicle. The rating does not have so much to do with the condition of the machine, but is based mostly on its uniqueness and desirability as indicated:

★★★★★ Five Stars—the best investment. To be given a five-star rating, a tractor must be historically significant. That is, it should be the first or last of a production sequence, an experimental model, a model with a limited production run, or a model that (because of age or attrition) has become unique. A five-star rating assumes an impeccable restoration, but even if not restored, the investment potential is there. These tractors are rare and expensive (unless the present owner is unaware of what he or she has). Because of this rarity, continued appreciation that should far outstrip inflation can be expected. Most often, major collectors know the existence and location of five-star tractors. These are sold or traded without the general public or lesser collectors being aware of their availability.

Melvin Ackman is shown on his 1924 Fordson at the 1993 Sycamore (Illinois) Show. The mounted Detroit mower was used in northern Wisconsin for cutting hemp. Its 7ft length was reduced to its present length of 5ft to lessen the sideload on the Fordson. Ackman is from Crystal Lake, Illinois.

★★★★ Four Stars—excellent investment potential. Four-star-rated tractors are still quite expensive, but appreciation should continue to exceed inflation. To be given a four-star rating, tractors must meet the same requirements as the five-star tractors, but to a lesser extent. The break between four and five stars is open to interpretation and is, of course, subjective. The same is true of the lower ratings.

★★★ Three Stars—very good investments if ownership satisfaction is considered. These are less expensive to buy than four- or five-star-rated tractors and will appreciate at a slower rate. On a three-star tractor, inflation will just about equal appreciation. These tractors represent the best compromise between desirability and cost.

★★ Two Stars—good investments, but with cost of ownership. These are tractors that are too new, or were produced in such numbers that they have not yet developed an appreciation history.

★ One Star—marginal investments. Tractors so new or so common, or that have been modified to such an extent that they have no antique value, rate one star. Also in this category are tractors built without equipment, such as hy-draulics, that were generally available for the type, and tractors with such bad reputations that they have no nostalgic value. Bear in mind that such reputations fade with time and as the majority of one-star machines get scrapped, the remainder move up in the star ratings. One-star tractors are for those who have storage space and are into collecting for the long haul.

Class Rating System

Another type of rating system is the class system that antique and collectible car people use to define the condition and state of restoration of their vehicles. This system is especially helpful in over-the-phone dealings, or in collector magazine sales advertisements:

Class 1—excellent. Class 1 tractors have been restored to current professional standards in every area or are completely original. All components operate like new. In all appearances, these tractors are brand new and unused. In other words, "Concours Condition."

Class 2—fine. Tractors categorized as Class 2 include well restored or superior restorations along with excellent originals or extremely well-maintained originals showing minimal wear.

Serial numbers 357 (left) and 364 (right) from the Fossum collection both have cast aluminum hoods. Serial number 364 has the optional tall air cleaner intake stack.

Early 9Ns show few differences over later Ford-Fergusons, but they are there. Note the smooth rear axle hubs. Also barely visible above the front wheel is a smaller-diameter two-pole generator. The semi-horizontal spoke aluminum grille was used through 1940.

Class 3—very good. The Class 3 rating is used for a completely operable original tractor, an older restoration now showing wear, or an amateur restoration not quite up to professional standards. It is presentable and serviceable inside and out, but not a Class 1 or 2. Also in this class are good partial restorations with parts to complete, and other variations on the theme.

Class 4—good. Class 4 tractors are operable or need minor work to become operable. Also included are deteriorated or poorly accomplished restorations and those in need of complete restoration. Generally, a Class 4 tractor is one that is, or has recently been, used for work and has not been refurbished.

Class 5—restorable. Tractors rated Class 5 need complete restoration. They may or may not be driveable, but are not weathered, wrecked, or stripped to the point of being useful only for salvage.

Be aware that there are two definite approaches to restoring old tractors: restoring to original or refurbishing to serviceable. Any tractor with a three-star or higher rating should be restored, and the class system presumes that such is the case. It is a travesty to carelessly refurbish, rather than restore, a valuable antique. Even with one- and two-star tractors, consideration should be given before originality is sacrificed, knowing that someday you, or someone else, may want to return it to its original state. Examples are conversion to a twelve-volt electrical system, or cutting off the steel rims to substitute them for rubber tires.

As is often true with Ford-built tractors from 1939 on, they are so useful as working tractors that thoughts of them as antiques are quickly stifled. Over the years parts are substituted from other models and all recollection of originality is lost. Such is the case with my own Ford-Ferguson. It is mostly a 2N, but has the rear axle of a 9N. It also has a 9N radiator. Someday I hope to swap some parts with Palmer Fossum and make it into the 2N it is supposed to be. But meanwhile, I can't be without it long enough to think about originality.

—*Robert N. Pripps*

Chapter 1

Henry Ford and the Farmer

The story of Ford tractors is really the story of Henry Ford. It's the story of an American farm boy who became one of the richest men of modern times. Within his eighty-three years, he touched more lives than any man of this century. In fact, he more than touched lives. Henry Ford changed the way people lived. This was especially true of the American farmer. It was Ford's desire, as he stated it, "To lift the burden of farming from flesh and blood and place it on steel and motors."

The story of the Ford-built tractor begins on July 30, 1863, when Henry was born to William and Mary Litogot Ford in Springwell Township, Wayne County, at Ford Road and Greenfield, near Detroit, Michigan. When his son Henry was born, William Ford, an Irish immigrant, was 38 years old and a successful agriculturist. Mary Litogot (O'Hern) was the adopted daughter of Patrick and Margaret O'Hern. Before Henry, William and Mary had had a stillborn child; three brothers and two sisters came after him. The family, including the O'Herns, lived in a frame house that William Ford had built. The house started with seven rooms, but ended up with eleven, expanding as the family grew.

William Ford grew wheat, corn, potatoes, and hay; tended horses, sheep, cows, and pigs; raised chickens for meat and eggs; cut wood; tended apple and peach orchards; smoked bacon and salted pork; grew vegetables in a large garden; tapped maples for sugar and syrup; made his own tools; and hunted, fished, trapped, and tanned animal skins.

The Ford women sewed, cooked, baked, churned, washed, made candles and soap, canned and preserved, knitted and gardened.

As young Henry grew up he was pressed into the duties around the farm. There is no question that farm work of the time was hard. (Farming is still hard work today, even with all the mechanical, electrical, and hydraulic aids.) His own early records indicate he never took to farm labor. "My earliest recollection," he later wrote, "is that there was too much work on the place." He also developed an aversion to chickens from his dealings with them as a lad, saying, "the chicken is fit only for hawks." This deep distaste for manual farm work spawned in young Henry an interest and instinct for machinery.

The Education of Henry Ford

Each year, there was time for schooling when things wound down after Christmas. Henry and the other farm children of the neighborhood would gather in the one-room schoolhouse. The McGuffey Readers reinforced the morals, conscience, self-reliance, and concept of duty to God and country that the Fords and other parents had instilled. Yet the sporadic schooling left Henry a poor written communicator and a worse speller. His schoolmasters and schoolmates undoubtedly also left their marks of influence. One schoolmate was Edsel Ruddiman, after whom Henry's only son would be named. Another, John Haggerty, said of their first teacher: "They used to pay the teacher $45 per month. But we used to need extra discipline. So they hired this cooper named J. B. Chapman and paid him $5 per month above the scale. That man could have told Henry and me all he knew in ten minutes. But he weighed 275 pounds and it was the weight that really counted."

Henry's father's hired hands also had an influence on young Henry and his mechanical aptitude. William Ford hired several German immigrants, refugees of the Franco-Prussian War of 1870. Their native Teutonic bent for things mechanical impressed the boy. One of these hired men went so far as to bring the lad a handful of clock and watch gears from a jeweler in Detroit, providing him with many hours of delight. Eventually, his family learned to guard clocks, watches, spring-wound toys, and the like from Henry's curiosity. As the years went on, he not only succeeded in taking these things apart, but also became able to put them back together. The next logical step was clock and watch repair, at which he became quite proficient. Henry claimed he fixed his first watch at age 13—and he made the tools he used in the repair.

Tools always were a fascination to Henry Ford. "They were my toys," he said in his 1922 autobiography, "and they still are."

Yet for all his aversion to the tedium of farm chores, Henry Ford was drawn to agriculture. Later, when he was successful and wealthy, he stated, "Growing of food, making of tools, and transportation are the three basic jobs!"

Steam Power

According to Henry Ford, the greatest experience of his young life was encountering a steam traction engine while traveling to Detroit with his father. (He said his second greatest experience was receiving the gift of a watch.)

"I was off the wagon and talking to the engineer before my father knew what I was up to," Ford wrote some forty-seven years later. "It was that engine which took me into automotive transportation. I eventually made a model of it that ran very well."

By the time Henry Ford was 16, he had left the farm for machine shop work in Detroit. During the next few years, he supplemented his income from the various machine shops by repairing watches in the evenings. When visiting home two years later in 1882, a neighbor came over and asked William Ford if he thought young Henry could get a steam engine running. It seems the neighbor had hired a threshing outfit and the engineer was having trouble with the new Westinghouse engine. In fact, the engineer was afraid of it and had quit. Henry got the engine going all right, and spent the rest of the season as its engineer. Later, he became a traveling serviceman for Westinghouse.

During this time, Henry had his first "tractor" experience. He built his own small steam engine from scratch; even casting the cylinder. He mounted this engine on a running gear supported by some discarded mower wheels. Unfortunately, the machine could only develop enough power to propel itself for 40 feet (ft). Still, for a man of 20, with only the crudest of tools and facilities, this was quite an accomplishment.

This 1926 ad extols the Fordson as the greatest time-saver in the hay field.

Business School

It was at this time that Henry undertook more schooling. He enrolled in Goldsmith's, Bryant and Stratton Business University in Detroit. He only attended the university for a few months, but between McGuffey and Goldsmith's, Henry learned to handle himself in the most complex business dealings. (It was said that he was never outwitted in a business deal in his life. Yet he and his company survived many financial crises.)

Henry Ford Grows Up

Sometime in 1885, Henry Ford was called to repair an Otto engine; a 4-cycle gasoline engine. Although it was the first one he had seen, he effected the repair. It was at that time he became infected with the gas engine bug that was to shape the rest of his life.

Later that year, he set up a sawmill on a wooded forty of land his father had given him upon turning 21. He cleared the timber and sawed boards for sale. During the next five years, he sawed 200,000 board feet of lumber. When he was not cutting timber, he was tinkering with gas en-

The greatest experience of Henry Ford's early life, as he stated in his autobiography, was seeing this steam traction engine on the road to Detroit. Forty-seven years later, he said that he remembered the event "like it was yesterday."

gines of his own design and construction. When Henry married Clara Jane Bryant in 1888, the young couple made their home in the small house on the acreage.

In 1891 Henry and Clara Ford moved to Detroit. Henry had taken a job at the Edison Illuminating Company as an engineer. Within three months, because of his ingenious handling of his duties, his pay was up to $50 per month—quite a handsome amount for that period. The engineering duties afforded time to tinker with gas engines, when the dynamos were all up and running. Besides, Henry always had a shop at home.

Gasoline Buggies

Two births occurred in the Ford household in late 1893. First, son Edsel was born on November 6; second, Henry Ford's first gasoline engine was "born" shortly thereafter. The engine roared to life clamped to the kitchen sink of the Ford home. Ford immediately set about the construction of a vehicle, which first ran on the streets of Detroit on June 4, 1896. It was named the "Quadricycle" because it resembled a four-wheeled bicycle. Henry Ford, now 33 years old, used it for awhile and then sold it for $200.

By 1899, Ford was at last ready to enter the vehicle business. The Detroit Automobile Company was organized and chartered on July 24 with the

papers being formally filed on August 5. Ten days later, Henry quit his post at Edison. Now, at last, Henry Ford had bet his life on his ideas about motor vehicles and business.

There were still some deep chuck holes on the road to success, however. The Detroit Automobile Company failed before the year was out. Why? Extant reports blame Henry, of all people, for failing to freeze his design and get the vehicle into production.

Ford escaped the collapse of the Detroit Automobile Company with enough resources to continue tinkering. He next went into racing, developing some highly successful cars. The engines powering these cars were an amazing 1,156 cubic inches (ci) in displacement.

In late 1901, the Henry Ford Company was organized to pick up where the Detroit Automobile Company left off. Again, things didn't work out for Henry and he resigned in 1902. After making twenty cars, the Henry Ford Company was reorganized into the Cadillac Automobile Company.

The Ford Motor Company

Finally, on June 16, 1903, the Ford Motor Company was organized. Henry Ford held 25.5 percent of the stock. The first product was a two-cylinder open carriage called the Ford Model A.

Henry Ford's first automobile, October 1896. It was powered by a four-cycle two-cylinder engine of 62ci. The pistons operated in unison so that there was a power stroke every revolution. The car had no reverse and no brakes. To back up, Ford merely got out and pushed it back. To stop, he killed the ignition and let compression bring it to a halt. The doorbell, on the front center of the car, was activated by a button on the tiller. It would not be long, however, before someone would find it difficult to take a photograph of the streets of Detroit and not get automobile traffic in the background.

Apparently, Henry had learned well the lesson about shooting the engineers and freezing the design, as more than 1,700 cars were completed in the next sixteen months. The twelve original stockholders, including Henry Ford, now 40 years old, split up a $100,000 dividend!

By 1905, the Ford Motor Company was turning out twenty-five Model B (four-cylinder) and Model C (two-cylinder) cars per day. By mid-1906, production was up to one hundred cars per day. As soon as the company was running smoothly, Ford's thoughts returned to the plight of the farmer. His interest, he said in an interview, was, "To make farming what it ought to be, the most pleasant and profitable profession in the world."

The Automobile Plow

Work on the first prototype Automobile Plow began in 1906, according to Charles Sorensen, who had joined the Ford Motor Company in 1905. The Auto-plow, as Ford called it, was powered by a 24hp Model B four-cylinder vertical engine. It utilized the Model B planetary transmission and radiator. Surviving reports indicate that this tractor lacked power, overheated, and had inadequate traction. Nevertheless, twelve variations on the basic theme were built and tested in 1907. An important note here is that the Auto-plow weighed less than 2,000lb. The more-or-less successful tractors of the day weighed ten times that much. Apparently, Ford already had his eye on the goal of creating a lightweight machine.

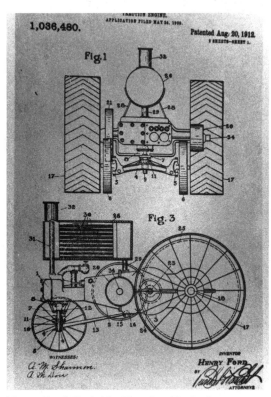

Henry Ford filed this "Traction Engine" patent application in 1908. The configuration was not unlike that of the successful Hart-Parr introduced in 1906. There is evidence that Ford began experimenting with farm tractors shortly after he formed the Ford Motor Company in 1903.

Auto Pull

PATENTED

Turns Your FORD into a GUARANTEED POWERFUL FARM TRACTOR

for Only $225

UNNECESSARY TO REMOVE WHEELS OR FENDERS WHEN TURNING YOUR FORD INTO AN AUTO PULL TRACTOR

CHANGES FORD to TRACTOR IN TEN MINUTES, and BACK TO PLEASURE CAR IN FIVE MINUTES

The Original Tractor Attachment
Weight of 1000 Lbs.
Assures Proper Traction
Notice The Sturdy Construction

Does The Work of 4 to 5 Horses At The Cost of One

Productive Advertising Campaign Is Making Sales for You Now

Our extensive farm paper advertising is bringing in thousands of inquiries from farmers in the states of Illinois, Minnesota, North and South Dakota, Montana, Idaho, Wisconsin, Iowa, Nebraska, Missouri and others. These thousands of farmers have been convinced of the superiority and advantages of owning an Auto Pull. Orders are coming in from these farmers every day some of them from your territory. You should be cashing in NOW. We create the demand—you make the sales. Mail the attached coupon for our Special Money-making Proposition for you.

Exceptional Profits for You Now

Now is the right time to take on the Auto Pull. Sales are going fine, and you will cash in big if you act at once. Take on this wonderful machine the price is right we can make prompt deliveries and furthermore you are taking on a machine that has stood up under all conditions for more than two years.

Mail Coupon for Dealer Proposition

Get our money-making proposition to dealers now. Make money while the time is right. Get the agency while your territory is still open. Tomorrow may be too late. Mail the coupon for full particulars today.

THE AUTO PULL COMPANY, Inc.
199 Franklin Street, Glencoe, Minn.

Features That Make the Auto Pull A Big, Easy Seller

The AUTO PULL Tractor Attachment is making a big success everywhere. It is built like a tractor, works like a tractor, and is a real powerful, sturdy machine, that will stand up well along side of the best tractors built. Once you see the Auto Pull working, its simple, sturdy construction, the ease with which the engine works, and the quickness in which you can turn a Ford into a tractor, you will be convinced of every claim we make for it.

No Wheels or Fenders to Remove

This is one of the Auto Pull's many exclusive features and one that is a big factor in making sales. The tractor wheels are forged steel (not cast). The special pulley attachment turns it into a powerful stationary gasoline engine that is worth the price of the entire tractor attachment alone.

The Auto Pull Company, Inc.,
199 Franklin Street, Glencoe, Minn.

Send me at once for my immediate consideration, full information regarding dealer proposition on Auto Pull Tractor Attachment.

Name ....

City .... State............

My Business Is ....

Territory Wanted................................

One of the many Model T tractor conversions that were on the market prior to the advent of the Fordson. *Smithsonian Photo*

The year 1908 saw twelve more variations of the Auto-plow built. Henry Ford also applied for his first traction engine patent that year (it was granted in 1912). That first patented design appears to be a departure from the lightweight concept, although it is difficult to tell from the patent drawing. The machine would have had a two-cylinder horizontal (side-by-side) engine. It would have used exhaust-induced cooling of the radiator, and probably would have been oil-cooled. It would have been much like the Hart-Parr, Rumely, or International Harvester tractors of that time. On October 1, 1908, the Ford Motor Company introduced the world-famous Model T car.

Tractor experiments seem to have been diminished somewhat for the next several years as the Model T was developed into the "Universal Car." Production of the car rose steadily from year to year, but it was 1914 that became pivotal in the history of the company. Three significant events happened that year. First, the $5.00 daily pay rate was established January 12 for Ford production work-

ers. This was an increase from the previous rate of $2.30 per day.

Second, and just as startling to the business community as the $5.00 daily pay rate, was the institution of the Model T moving assembly line on January 14.

Third, the turmoil in Europe boiled over after the assassination of Archduke Ferdinand, and in August, Germany declared war on Russia and France; World War I had begun.

World War I

The effect of these three events caused car production at Ford to skyrocket. The war increased demand for US farm products, and the tractor industry began to expand dramatically as well. With the car business again solid, Henry Ford turned his attention once more to tractors. Although he had the financial resources and the technical talent, Ford's fellow directors did not share his enthusiasm for the tractor business. Nevertheless, research continued in 1914 and

A Model T-based experimental tractor plowing at Henry Ford's farm in 1915. The left tank contained water to supplement that in the radiator; the right tank held the gasoline. A double reduction worm-drive rear end was used, as was the Model T planetary transmission.

1915 on tractors based on Model T components. The popularity of the Model T with the farmers had spawned a plethora of tractor conversions. C. H. Wendel's *Encyclopedia of American Farm Tractors* lists no fewer than forty-five companies making Model T-to-tractor conversion kits at about this time. While some of these worked out fairly well, others did not. Ford never discouraged these conversions, but basked in the notoriety they engendered.

Henry Ford, Pacifist

Henry Ford was widely known as a pacifist for his much-criticized "Peace Ship" activities of 1915. The truth was, however, that while he was against war, he was, as he said in 1915, willing to fight for peace:

"My opposition to war is not based on pacifist, or non-resistant principles. It may be that our present state of civilization is such that certain international questions cannot be discussed; it may be that they have to be fought out. But the fighting never settles the question. It only gets the participants around to a frame of mind where they will agree to discuss what they were fighting about."

Fordson prototype X-6 shown in a photo dated July 1917. It closely resembled production Fordsons. Note that it is nameless at this point.

The Farkas Design

In the summer of 1916, prototypes of a new Ford tractor were shown to the public and caused quite a stir among farmers. No longer was this a Model T derivative, but an entirely new concept. The engine block, transmission housing, and rear axle housing were the frame of the machine. The father of the design was Eugene Farkas, who had the benefit of the convenient test fields of Ford's newly acquired Fair Lane Estate. He was also able to try out just about every make of tractor.

Work on the design had started in 1915 using a Hercules-made engine. This tractor evolved into one closely resembling the production Fordson. Prior to the US press showing, two tractors were sent to England for testing by the British government. These were the first to bear the name badge "Henry Ford and Son."

Tractor work was now being done in a separate factory utilizing Henry Ford's, not Ford Motor Company's, funds. Henry Ford was now 53 years old; son Edsel was 23. A new private company, Henry Ford and Son, Inc., was incorporated July 27, 1917, for the express purpose of mass producing the new low-cost tractor.

The Ford Motor Company still had non-Ford family stockholders at the time, and Henry chafed under their restrictions. Rather than gain their permission for the tractor venture, he simply formed a new company. He was prevented from calling the new company "The Ford Tractor Company" because a Minneapolis, Minnesota, outfit already had usurped that name. The Minneapolis company *did* actually include a man whose last name was "Ford," but naming the company for him seemed like a blatant effort to capitalize on Henry Ford's fame. The Minneapolis-based Ford Tractor Company did actually sell a few tractors, but extant reports indicate they were completely unsatisfactory.

The World War I Food Problem

Britain, and indeed much of Western Europe, had come to rely on imported grain from the United States, Canada, Australia, and Russia. The low cost of these foods caused Britain's farmers to turn to livestock production. When the Turkish Navy blockaded the Dardanelles in 1914, they effectively shut off the flow of wheat from Russia. Later, the German U-boat threat began to curtail grain shipments from the other sources. The British government reacted by establishing tilling goals for arable acreage. Records indicate there were just 500 tractors in Great Britain in 1914. To achieve their tillage goals, the British Board of Agriculture ordered tractors from British makers to the limit of

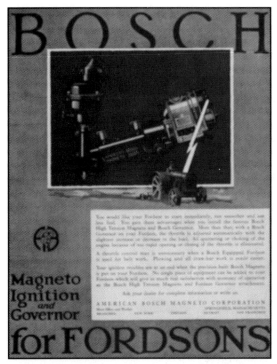

The Model T type coil ignition was always the bane of the Fordson. Here, American Bosch advertises its high-tension magneto conversion.

their production capacity. They also ordered the importing of all the Waterloo Boys and International Harvesters they could get, but still food production fell short.

Fortunately for all concerned, Lord Percival Perry was the chief of Ford's British subsidiary and also a member of the Board of Agriculture. It was Lord Perry who arranged for testing of the Ford's prototype tractors in May 1916. A panel of five judges, all experienced agriculturists, were favorably impressed by the Ford tractor's durability, ease in starting and handling, and its small size and light weight. They recommended that the British Ford subsidiary go into immediate production. Ford had previously been granted a license to set up a factory in Cork, Ireland, to produce the Model T, and that site was chosen for tractor production. Henry Ford was delighted, and generously made a gift of the drawings and patent rights for the duration of the conflict.

Thus, Henry Ford was finally in the tractor business. His intention was to begin production in Detroit, as well as in Cork. He was pleased and proud to include son Edsel in the business, and to get him started.

Chapter 2

The American Fordson

★★★★★ **X-Designs 1917 (Serial No. X-1 through X-15)**

★★★★★ **Ministry of Munitions (MOM) Tractors 1917-1918 (Serial No. 1 through approximately 3900)**

★★★★ **Fordson F 1918-1919: through Serial No. 88,088 (Dearborn); through Serial No. 65103 (Cork)**

★★★★ **Fordson F 1920-1923: through Serial No. 365191 (Dearborn and Detroit); through Serial No. 253552 (Cork)**

★★ **Fordson F 1924-1926; through Serial No. 629030 (Detroit)**

★★★ **Fordson F 1927; through Serial No. 747681**
★★★★ **Serial No. 747682 and up**

In 1916, the Farkas-design experimental tractors were demonstrated to the British. The success of these machines resulted in an immediate order for production in the United Kingdom.

German bombing of London and other English cities in June 1917 forced a revision of Ford's Cork, Ireland, production plans. All resources were now needed to make war machines, such as fighter planes, for the defense of the country. Tractors would have to be imported. On June 28, 1917, Henry Ford announced that he had accepted an order for 6,000 tractors from the British Ministry of Munitions (MOM); they would be built in the United States.

Between the time the order was accepted and October 8, when production started, the design was overhauled. As many as fifteen X-models were built and tested, each one progressively more like the production tractor. In the process, the car-type radiator was increased in size so that its capacity was 11 gallons (gal); this cured overheating problems. The larger radiator also added weight to the front to help hold down the tractor. Next, the worm drive in the rear end was relocated. It had been on top, under the seat. During heavy operation the heat became unbearable to the operator. Revising the design to put the worm below solved the problem of the hot seat and also allowed for larger rear wheels. Thus another problem was overcome, that of inadequate traction. Finally, several changes were made to improve ease of production. The Fordson would use the Model T coil magneto system. Water and oil pumps would be eliminated in favor of the simpler thermocycle cooling and splash lubrication.

Before the end of 1917, 254 MOM tractors were completed. These as yet had no Fordson identification and were hence given the MOM nickname for the Ministry of Munitions contract. The name "Fordson" actually came from the transatlantic cable address and was a contraction of "Henry Ford and Son." In those days, transatlantic communication was laborious and slow and done in Morse code. Hence, names were shortened and acronyms were used wherever possible. Tractors were not formally called Fordsons until the MOM order was completed and production for the general public started.

Production problems plagued the new assembly line at the Dearborn, Michigan, plant and deliveries were way behind schedule. Nevertheless, production got on track in 1918. The 6,000 tractors amounted to less than sixty days of production, although actual deliveries took somewhat longer. Because of shipping limitations, many were not delivered to England but to Canada and other Commonwealth locations. Production Fordsons filled the balance of the MOM order.

Enter the Fordson

On June 26, 1918, the US Department of Agriculture granted a license to Henry Ford and Son for the manufacture of tractors for the American market. A total of 34,167 Fordsons were built in 1918. With the end of World War I, plans to build the Fordson in Ireland were revived, and the first Cork-built Fordson came off the line on July 4, 1919. US tractor production was transferred from the Dearborn plant to the River Rouge plant during the winter of 1920-1921. Now Fordson production could reach the mass production scale originally envisioned by Henry Ford.

The Great Twenties Tractor War: Birth of the General Purpose Tractor

"What? What's that? How much? Two hundred and thirty dollars? Well, I'll be... What'll we do about it? Do? Why damn it all, meet him, of course! We're going to stay in the tractor business. Yes, cut $230. Both models. Yes, both. And, say, listen, make it good! We'll throw in a plow as well."

That is one-half of a January 28, 1922, telephone conversation between International Harvester's Chicago and Springfield, Ohio, offices. The words are those of Alexander Legge, the company's gritty general manager as recorded by Cyrus McCormick III in his book *The Century of the Reaper*. The occasion was a salvo fired by Henry Ford in the great tractor war of the twenties. He had just announced a price cut to $395 for a Fordson tractor.

McCormick, grandson of the reaper inventor and then president of International Harvester also wrote, "The harvester war of the eighteen-nineties

Note the single fuel tank bung on this 1923 Fordson. Double-bung tanks appeared in 1924. Also note the low-bead front wheel, which was used until mid-1925, and the "Rainbow" coil box. This tractor is on display at Koller's Realty in Manitowish Waters, Wisconsin.

was cruel, disastrous to the weaker combatants, and yet it was inspiring in the way its testing brought out the finer qualities of men. [In the intervening years,] competition had perhaps become routine. Henry Ford's presence in the implement province and the new type of competition he soon introduced returned the industry for a time to the atmosphere of battle."

Trust Busting

Formed in 1902, International Harvester Company had been under constant legal attack from then until after World War I. This was an era when trust busting was a fashionable thing for politicians and lawyers. The merging of the several companies to form International Harvester was considered by some a patent attempt to eliminate competition. Several states, at least for a short time, forbade Harvester to do business within their borders. All this culminated about 1918 with the sale of three of the several companies making up International Harvester, and by the elimination of dual (McCormick and Deering) dealerships. Now, having survived all that, they found themselves under a strong competitive attack.

By the end of World War I, International Harvester's "full-line" competitors were proving increasingly able, especially in the tractor market. Chief competitors included Massey-Harris, Case, and Deere (just entering the tractor fray in 1919

This 1923 Fordson at Koller's Realty in northern Wisconsin has the starting gasoline tank mounted on the water-washer air cleaner. It also has the rubber steering wheel and a belt pulley.

World War I left Great Britain with an intense farm labor shortage. This, coupled with the fact that much of Europe's farmland was out of production due to the war, threatened dire food shortages in 1917. The British government sought ways to rapidly mechanize the country's farms. Aware of Ford's tractor development, a delegation was sent to the Ford farm to inspect the tractor. They must have been suitably impressed as 6,000 were brought over the next year.

with the purchase of the Waterloo Boy outfit). In addition, there were many short-line, or tractor-only competitors, including (in 1917) one Henry Ford of automobile fame.

Mass Production

Ford had an empathy with the hard-working, underpaid, and mostly unappreciated farmer. He was concerned especially for the eastern and mid-western small farmer trying to wrest a living often from less than 80 acres. Ford intended that his tractor would do for the farmer what his Model T car had done, that is, free him from bondage to the horse. By 1920, Fordson production was such that a month's output would exceed the total number of tractors of any of the other producers for the whole year.

Ford soon found himself, because of the post-war depression, with more tractors than could be sold. He started cutting prices to move inventory. The market in the early twenties continued to shrink, further exacerbating the then industry-wide overproduction problem. The other producers, eager to maintain market share, also cut prices, and soon found themselves embroiled in a good, old-fashioned price war.

The tractor price war had three prominent effects. First, many farmers took advantage of the below-cost prices to get into power farming. Second, substantial companies were eliminated from the tractor market when they could not get their prices down sufficiently to compete, mainly the "short-

The original small-lettered toolbox (above) was used through 1919. Thereafter, the large-lettered box was used.

line" companies specializing in larger, heavier tractors. Finally, the survivors were forced to copy Ford's production line methods and redesign their products to be more appealing to the myriad of

The ladder-side radiator shell was used into 1919. Thereafter, the shell was solid.

smaller farmers.

Farm Machinery and Equipment magazine listed 166 tractor companies in 1920. They produced just over 200,000 tractors. That year, Ford produced 67,000 Fordsons in Dearborn and 3,600 in Cork, Ireland.

When the Fordson was launched in 1918, the industry didn't take it seriously at first. Philip C. Rose, writer of the *Black Book*, dismissed the Fordson as inconsequential, saying the other tractor manufacturers need not worry about Ford. "His machine," Rose said of Ford's Fordson, "will not stand up; that he will find in short order."

The reasons for the disdain of the Fordson by the tractor gurus of the time were several. First, Ford's claim to fame was the Model T car. While the Model T put America on wheels, it was not a favorite of the automotive experts. One thing the tractor gurus missed, however, was that the Model T was a favorite of the small farmer. Also, many farmers thought of Henry Ford as a saint because of his $5.00-a-day pay policy.

Second, the Fordson was ridiculously small and light. At 2,700lb it was dwarfed by other new tractors of the times, such as the 6,000lb Waterloo Boy or the 8,700lb IHC Titan.

Finally, Ford was not in the farm implement business. The most prosperous tractor suppliers also made equipment such as threshers, spreaders, mowers, and the like. What the tractor gurus failed to anticipate was that Ford would distribute the tractors through his existing extensive automobile dealer network. He issued quotas for each; even big city dealers had to take their share, doing whatever they could to get rid of them.

Post-World War I Depression

In 1921, the post-war depression caused the downturn in sales from 71,000 to less than 37,000. Henry Ford's tractor "engine" was running, though, and a way had to be found to move more tractors. Thus the prices were cut throughout the year from $795 to $625, and finally the dramatic cut to $395. Now Fordsons sold. The year 1922 saw production back to around the 70,000 level, and in 1923, over 100,000 were sold.

International Harvester first countered with the 10-20 McCormick Deering in 1922, a smaller version of the 15-30 introduced in 1921. Others, such as Case and John Deere brought out new, smaller, lighter, less expensive models as well. Nevertheless, Ford claimed over 60 percent of the market. Competition from the Fordson eliminated many companies from the field over the next several years, including the mighty General Motors entry, the Samson.

By 1929, the great tractor war was over. There

were only 47 tractor manufacturers left of the 166 listed for 1920; they were still producing just a few over 200,000 units. By then, both the Fordson and the Model T were also gone from the scene. Henry Ford said he stopped production of the Fordson because he needed the space for construction of the new Model A car, brought out in 1928 to replace the Model T. But the facts are that the Fordson, as well as the Model T, had been overtaken by determined competition: In the case of the Model T, it was the Chevrolet automobile; in the case of the Fordson, it was the Farmall tractor International Harvester introduced in 1924.

Collecting Comments
X-Designs 1917; Serial No. X-1 through X-15

The X-designs were completely different from the MOM tractors and the later Fordson F. One or two are known to exist and are already in the hands of collectors. Early numbers may have been scrapped, or rebuilt and renumbered. It is not known for sure that there were fifteen of the X-models built, but that is the general consensus.

When Sorensen returned from England to set up production in Dearborn, Henry Ford would have delayed production in order to accommodate design changes. In October 1917, however, Lord North

A drawbar extension was a popular option as it allowed sharper turns without interference between the extended fenders and implements.

The three-hole drawbar-worm cover was used through 1920. Thereafter, the five-hole type was used. The center hole in both cases was originally like the others, but wear from use has elongated them. To the five-hole type, Ford added a large hole for hooking a chain.

This Fordson has aftermarket Weisel fenders. Note the fender mounting brackets. Such fenders were popular add-ons before Ford offered fenders as an option in 1923.

Two well-worn Fordson belt pulleys show early (right) and late mounting splines. The early type, which was subject to loosening up with wear, was used until 1920.

cliffe, a senior representative of the British government, arrived to influence Henry to cut off the X-models and get on with production. Thus, on October 8 the design was frozen and production began.

Experts believe the X-designs were made in pairs. X-1 and X-2 had separate rear-end and transmission castings like the earlier Farkas design, where X-3 and X-4 had one-piece housings. X-5 and X-6 were built in early August. These had belt pulleys, later discarded as not needed by the British, then to be revived for the F series as an option. X-7 and X-8 were built in mid-August and had wider rear wheels. Models X-9 and X-10 had magneto revisions; X-11 and X-12 had the final Fordson-type fuel tank, without hinges for side panels. X-13 through X-15, if they existed, were probably insurance models of the X-11 and X-12 designs so that more test hours could be built up before production got going.

Of course, there were other changes incorporated besides the ones listed for each X, but these are the ones visible in extant photos.

The Ministry of Munitions (MOM) Tractors 1917-1918; Serial No. 1 through approximately 3900

The MOM tractors were not yet Fordsons. In fact when the "Fordson" designation began to appear in April 1918, the MOM era was over. The first official Fordson F, built for Luther Burbank, rolled off the line on April 23. Thus the last half, approximately, of the MOM order for 6,000 tractors was filled during Fordson production.

Identifying characteristics of the MOM tractors include:
• Shallow-lid toolboxes with no logo
• Cast iron front wheel hubcaps
• Three-piece tie and steering rods
• 6-spoke rear wheels
• The gas tank had no logo and was rounder
• A blank fuel tank end and no top center seam
• No logo on the radiator tank
• Oil filler in rear of engine, held on with two bolts

Unfortunately because of the interchangeability requirements of mass production, these identifying parts may have been replaced by later Fordson parts—including the whole engine (which includes the serial number, a problem with all Ford-built tractors).

Otherwise, the MOM tractors were much like the pre-1920 Fordsons. There is some evidence that minor changes were incorporated on the line, and that the Fordson name began appearing on radiator tanks before the April 23 switch.

The Hadfield-Penfield Steel Company, of Bucyrus, Ohio, made these crawler half-tracks for Fordsons back in 1926. The tracks added 2,500lb to the Fordson's weight.

Characteristics of the X-Design and MOM tractors:
Engine: Hercules-built, 4x5in bore and stroke,
   251ci, four-cylinder, L-head, rated at 1000rpm
Weight: About 2,500lb, growing to 2,700lb
Transmission: Three speeds forward, one reverse
Final Drive: Worm and wheel
Color: Olive gray with oxide red wheels

The Fordson F 1918-1919; through
Serial No. 88088 (Dearborn); through
Serial No. 65103 (Cork)

The MOM tractors started with Serial Number 1 and continued through Serial Number 3900. There is then an unexplained gap in the numbering to Serial Number 6901. These units were built in mid-April 1918. About this same time, Henry Ford and Son received permission to supply tractors for the domestic market. The first ten tractors not produced for the Ministry of Munitions order were labeled "Fordson" on the radiator, fuel tank, and toolbox and were numbered 1 through 10. These first ten tractors were delivered to special friends of

Henry Ford. Number 1 (which now resides in the Henry Ford Museum) went to Luther Burbank, the botanist. Number 2 went to Thomas Edison.

After these first ten American Fordsons, the numbering system reverted to the sequence begun with the MOMs. Hercules was building and numbering engines and was too far ahead of tractor production to change. The company supplied some unnumbered engines for replacements of engines that, for some reason, didn't pass muster. The first ten Fordsons used these replacement engines hand-stamped with their 1 through 10 numbers.

Between Serial Numbers 6901 and about 7260, produced in the last weeks of April 1918, Fordson Fs and MOMs were mixed on the assembly line. Tractors in this sequence can carry either label, depending upon whether or not they were for the United States and Canadian markets or for the Ministry of Munitions order.

In the summer of 1918, Fordson production for the US market was ready to take off. World

Marlo Remme shows the difference between the low-bead (left) and high-bead front Fordson wheels. Fordsons built prior to the 1926 model year used the low-bead type with the larger hub. Note the hubcap wrench in Remme's right hand.

The three types of Fordson ignition coil boxes. Originally, a Model T box (right) with special cast brackets was used into 1919. Next came the "rainbow" box, which used the same cover as the Model T. The rainbow box was used until 1925 when the final Fordson box (left) came out.

War I was still on, however, and farmers wanting to purchase new tractors of any kind had to obtain a permit from their local County War Board. Generally, a quota of 1,000 tractors for each agricultural state was established. Fordsons were sold through regular Ford car and truck dealers, although the Henry Ford and Son Company was still separate from the Ford Motor Company.

By mid-1918, Henry Ford and Son Company had a good handle on the cost to build Fordsons. The price, which probably included about 30 percent profit, was right at $795. As production methods improved and the daily production numbers went up, costs came down somewhat.

Production of the Fordson F began in the new plant in Cork, Ireland, on April 4, 1919. Only 300 Fordsons were completed that year, however.

Characteristics of 1918 and 1919 Fordson Tractors:
Engine: Hercules-built, 4x5in bore and stroke, 251ci, four-cylinder, L-head, rated at 1000rpm
Weight: 2,710lb
Transmission: Three speeds forward, one reverse
Final Drive: Worm and wheel
Color: Machinery gray with bright red wheels, 6-spoke rears, no fenders
Labeling: Ladder-side radiator cover with "Fordson" cast on the front (this logo was implemented by a temporary insert, and can be quite irregular, tilted, etc.). "Manufactured by Henry Ford and Son" on the rear of the tank
Model T coil box with cast brackets
Round axle housings without grooves; no fenders or fender mounting provisions
Maple wood steering wheel (like Model T)
Round holes in pressed steel seat
Three-hole drawbar

The Fordson F 1920-1923; through Serial Number 365191 (Dearborn and Detroit); through Serial Number 253552 (Cork)

Toward the end of 1919, Henry Ford established the Eastern Holding Company, a Delaware corporation, for the purpose of acquiring all the minority stock in the Ford Motor Company. With family capital of over $100 million, Eastern Holding procured the assets of the Ford Motor Company, Henry Ford and Son, Inc., and other Ford business interests. In early 1920, when these activities were completed, the Eastern Holding name was dropped in favor of the Michigan-chartered Ford Motor Company.

Now freed of stockholder control, Henry Ford was able to move toward his goal of manufacturing vehicles from raw materials, rather than by purchasing sub-assemblies from suppliers.

A two-compartment (double-bung) fuel tank was introduced for the Fordson in 1924. Previously, the gasoline tank had been bolted to the water-washer tank at the holes shown. Water-washer tanks continued to have the holes until the supply was used up. This photo shows the gas line passing by on its way to the carburetor.

A 1924 Fordson "Industrial." Note the special wheels and hard rubber tires.

One of his first moves was the construction of the giant River Rouge plant outside Detroit.

The Rouge plant contained its own powerhouse, steel smelting plant, and ship-docking facility. Fordson production was terminated at the Brady Street plant in Dearborn and transferred to the new Rouge plant. From the 1920 model and on, the stamping on the end of the fuel tank reads "Manufactured by Ford Motor Company, Detroit, Michigan [or Cork, Ireland]."

In late 1920, a severe downturn occurred in the world's economy due to production adjustments required (but not made) at the end of World War I. This couldn't have come at a worse time for the over-extended Fords. Further exacerbating the problem was a six-month interruption in Fordson production due to the factory move from Dearborn to Rouge.

Steps were taken by all divisions to cut costs and boost sales. The price of the Fordson was cut

Marlo Remme's 1926 Fordson has the extended
drawbar and square-tail fenders.

109070

ILLINOIS PRAIRIE DISTRICT LIBRARY

to $625, and quotas were established for dealers. When many of the other farm implement and tractor companies followed suit in price cutting, Ford administered the coup de grace to many of them by further cutting the Fordson price to $395. This touched off the Great Twenties Tractor War mentioned earlier in the chapter.

When production was up to speed at the River Rouge plant in 1922, production was discontinued at the Cork, Ireland, plant and at the newly instituted Hamilton, Ohio, plant. Also in 1922 a prototype Fordson 2-ton truck was built. It was to be a conventional heavy duty truck with the 25ci Fordson engine. Apparently, bad economic times spelled doom for the Fordson truck.

Characteristics of the Fordson F 1920-1923:
Engine: Ford-built, 4x5in bore and stroke, 251ci, four-cylinder, L-head, rated at 1000rpm
Weight: 2,710lb
Transmission: Three speeds forward, one reverse

Final Drive: Worm and wheel. 1922 and on, it had a double-lead worm.
Brakes: None until 1923, then a transmission disk brake clutch pedal-operated
Color: Machinery gray with bright red wheels, 7-spoke; rears, no fenders
Labeling: Solid-side radiator cover with "Fordson" cast on the front with "permanent" casting insert. "Manufactured by Ford Motor Company" on the rear of the tank
"Rainbow" coil box
Round axle housings without grooves, no fenders or fender mounting provisions
Maple wood steering wheel (like Model T)
Slotted holes in pressed steel seat
Five-hole drawbar
Two oil drain plugs (one for dirt trap)
Toolbox with large "Fordson" and extended flanges on cover

Characteristics of later American Fordson Fs are shown here. After 1920, writing on the end of the fuel tank read, "Fordson—manufactured by Ford Motor Company—Detroit, Michigan." The large-lettered toolbox (1919), double-bung tank (1924), and fender brackets (1923) are also shown.

This Kingston Regenerator carburetor-manifold setup is typical of the later Fordsons.

Fordson F 1924-1926; through Serial No. 629030 (Detroit)

The Fordson tractor was essentially a mature item by 1924. The Ford Motor Company was also hitting its stride by that year, the financial troubles of 1921 and 1922 behind it. In fact, 1923 Fordson production had set a record for tractor production of 101,898 units (surpassed only by Fordson in 1925). In 1924, 900 Fordsons were sent to the Soviet Union, and eventually, 25,000 would follow. During 1925, the 500,000th Fordson was built and an unsurpassed tractor model production record of 104,168 was set.

With the addition of the transmission brake in 1923, the use of hard rubber-tired industrial Fordsons proliferated. One, with a front-mounted sweeper, was even said to be owned by GM to sweep their walks.

The appearance was changed by the use of a lighter gray paint, and by the availability of optional fenders starting in 1924. In 1925, the tool-box fenders, sometimes called orchard fenders, were made available. Besides a handy place to store

The flip-up cover on the oil filler first appeared on Fordsons in 1923.

tools, these fenders were supposed to prevent rearing accidents, for which Fordsons were becoming infamous.

Also in 1925 and 1926, a plethora of aftermarket variations on the Fordson theme appeared. There were graders, road rollers, golf course mowers, and the like. One of the most unique was the Trackson, built by the Full Crawler Company of Milwaukee, Wisconsin. This conversion, popular with loggers, made the Fordson into a track-layer. Over 88,000 were converted before the company was bought by Caterpillar.

Characteristics of the Fordson F 1924-1926:
Engine: Ford-built, 4x5in bore and stroke, 251ci, four-cylinder, L-head, rated at 1000rpm
Weight: 2,970lb
Transmission: Three speeds forward, one reverse
Final Drive: Worm and wheel, double-lead worm
Brakes: Transmission disk brake clutch pedal-operated

Color: Light gray with bright red wheels, 7-spoke rear wheels, fenders optional
Labeling: Solid-side radiator cover with "Fordson" cast on the front with "permanent" casting insert. "Manufactured by Ford Motor Company" on the rear of the tank
"Rainbow" coil box; new Fordson box in 1925
Hard rubber steering wheel
Five-hole drawbar
Two oil drain plugs (one for dirt trap)
Two-bung fuel tank (gas starting tank internal, eliminating the cast gas tank bolted to the water washer)
Model T type oil breather
Oil filler had flip-up cover
High bead front wheels

Fordson F 1927; through Serial No. 747681

At the Ford Motor Company, 1927 was an unusual year because the company did not introduce any new models. General Motors, especially

This Fordson has an aftermarket water pump, which was patented in June 1919.

Chevrolet, had been coming on strong as a competitor. Ford car and truck sales were declining rapidly, and much of the technical talent was tied up developing the new Model A line. In midyear, car and truck production was terminated. This left most dealers without much to sell except for the Fordson tractor. Thus, even though its US production days were numbered, the Fordson enjoyed a good year with production (which actually ended in 1928) of 101,973 units. Approximately 8,000 of these were built in what would be the 1928 model year, but most enthusiasts consider them late-built 1927 models. Any Fordson with a Serial Number above 747,500 should be given a five-star rating, if it was built in Detroit.

The new Model A was to be built on such a scale that the production facilities of the Fordson tractor were needed. Ford could also see that the appetite of the American farmer was changing for tractors. The Farmall introduced in 1924 had revo-lutionized their thinking just as the Fordson had in 1917. The Farmall was the result of many years of development by the International Harvester Research Department, which sought a machine for motorized crop cultivation. The configuration finally decided upon was the first to use what has come to be known as the "row crop" setup. It had dual narrow front wheels that ran between the rows, and wide-spread, large-diameter rear wheels that straddled the rows. The high rear axle gave ample crop clearance. The Farmall could do crop cultivation as well as the traditional jobs of the tractor on the farm, and thus was the first all-purpose, or general purpose, tractor.

Ford realized that his profit potential would be continuously squeezed by these new competitive row-crop tractors unless he undertook a new design. He had, however, his hands full with the new car and truck line.

In December 1928, Ford transferred control of

Marlo Remme and his "pulling tractor," a 1925 Fordson with old-style fenders. It also has a battery box to ease starting, rubber tires, and lots of wheel weights. In addition, it has a Ford optional gasoline head and an aftermarket manifold setup. Remme says he's been doing quite well in competition. His dad bought the tractor in 1948.

Marlo Remme shows proper cranking form in starting his 1921 Fordson. Note the Model T type coil box, not correct for this year, but handy because of the convenient key. Remme's sons are in the trucking business.

Ford Motor Company (England) Ltd. and Henry Ford and Son, Ltd., of Cork, to British citizens and to a new company, Ford Motor Company, Ltd. Worldwide rights to the Fordson tractor were assigned to the new company. In 1928, all production tooling was transferred to Cork.

Characteristics of the Fordson F 1927:
Engine: Ford-built, 4x5in bore and stroke, 251ci, four-cylinder, L-head, rated at 1000rpm. Revised engine block with lower manifold and more water around valves
Weight: 3,000lb
Transmission: Three speeds forward, one reverse
Final Drive: Worm and wheel, double-lead worm.
Brakes: Transmission disk brake clutch pedal-op-erated, industrial version available with pneumatic tires and wheel brakes
Color: Light gray with bright red wheels, 7-spoke rears, tapered tool-box fenders optional
Labeling: Solid-side radiator cover with "Fordson" cast on the front with "permanent" casting insert. "Manufactured by Ford Motor Company" on the rear of the tank
New Fordson coil box (cover shared with Model T)
Hard rubber steering wheel
Five-hole drawbar, extension optional
Two oil drain plugs (one for dirt trap)
Two-bung fuel tank (gas starting tank internal)
Model T type oil breather
Oil filler had flip-up cover

The absence of a steering wheel on this Fordson crawler conversion makes it easier to see the logo stamping on the rear of the fuel tank.

High bead front wheels
Fordson F Model Serial Numbers

Year	US Production	Irish Production
1917	1 to 259	
1918	260 to 29979	
1919	34427 to 88088	63001 to 63200
		65001 to 65103
1920	100001 to 158178	65104 to 65500
		105001 to 108229
1921	158312 to 170891	108230 to 109672
1922	201026 to 262825	109673 to 110000
		170958 to 172000
		250001 to 250300
		253001 to 253552
1923	268583 to 365191	
1924	370351 to 448201	
1925	455360 to 549901	
1926	557608 to 629030	
1927 and		
1928	629830 to 747681	

The Fordson vs. the Mule

Charles Domeier, of Pecatonica, Illinois, recounts the following tale:

"When I was a lad, my father farmed in Nebraska. We had farmed with mules until one day Dad came home with a new Fordson. We had two ground-driven binders of about the same size. He hooked one to the Fordson and the other to a team of four mules. He got on the Fordson and gave me the binder and the mules and we headed for the field. During that day, I and the mules passed the Fordson four times!"

★★★★	Cork Fordson N, Serial No. 747682-779135
★★★	Dagenham Fordson N 1933-1945, Serial No. 779154-980519, Regulars
★★★★	Dagenham Fordson N 1933-1945, Serial No. 779154-980519, All-Arounds

Fordsons from Cork and Dagenham

This is an orange 1939 Fordson N Standard that was restored by its owner, Keith Dorey of Wareham, Dorset. It is shown at the 1993 Great Dorset Steam Fair.

Fordson production ceased in Detroit in mid-1928. In ten years, almost 850,000 had hit the fields. But the versatility, traction, and reliability of the new breed of small row-crop tractors from IHC, Hart-Parr, and others doomed the Fordson. It needed a complete update, similar to the change between the Model T and Model A cars.

Ford had discussed such a change, but before anything definitive occurred, the world's economy was hit with the Great Depression. The Depression began with the Crash of '29 but the effects, especially for the farmer, were not felt until 1931. Coupled with high unemployment was a lack of credit and severe drought. These factors soon held the tractor market almost to a standstill.

The decision to transfer tractor operations to Ford Motor Company, Ltd., was at the request of Ford's influential friend Lord Percival Perry, who was heading up the new company (formed by consolidating Dagenham and Cork operations). Even in 1928 things were tough in the European car and truck markets, and Lord Perry reasoned that even the spares business for existing Fordsons would be a shot in the arm. Further, the Soviet Union had tried to order more Fordsons to augment the 25,000 they already had, but were turned down when Detroit production was terminated. The Soviets then turned to International Harvester and placed a substantial order. Sir Perry reasoned that more Soviet orders would be forthcoming.

Because of the economic slowdown and because it was going to take more than six months to move the lines to Cork, Ford Motor Company, Ltd., decided to upgrade and improve the Fordson within its basic design. By the time production started in early 1929, numerous back orders had been built up. Some construction operations in building the new Fordson, called the Model N, were completed outside as the machinery had not yet been moved in.

The most important change made for the Irish N was in the engine. First, the bore was increased 0.125in, making it 267ci, rather than the 251ci of the Fordson F. Next, a high-tension impulse-coupling conventional magneto replaced the Model T coils. The performance of aftermarket high-compression gasoline heads did not go unnoticed. The new Model N was available in either kerosene or gasoline versions. The University of Nebraska's conservative ratings for the two versions of the Model N were: 21hp (kerosene) and 26hp (gasoline) on the belt.

Instead of spoked front wheels, the new Model N had cast front wheels. It also had a heavier front axle with a downward bend in the middle and a larger water washer. The paint scheme remained the same, but the wing-type orchard fenders were standard. On the rear end of the fuel tank were the words "Ford Motor Company, Ltd., England, Made in Irish Free State." Some said "Made by Ford Motor Company, Ltd., Cork, Ireland."

The Move to Dagenham

The choice of Cork for a production facility had been at best based on Henry Ford's sentimentality and on his perceived need to "give something back to his roots." The cost of raw materials was high and the availability of skilled labor was low. Also, very few of the Fordsons built stayed in Ireland. This, coupled with some political problems, not to mention the distance from the London headquarters, made the Cork location less than optimum.

In 1929, Ford Motor Company, Ltd., began construction of a new factory complex in Dagenham, Essex, on the outskirts of London. By 1932 when the factory was completed, there was much excess capacity because of the continuing Depression. It was also in 1932 when Fordson production in Cork hit a low of fifty per week. Lord Perry approached Henry Ford about the possibility of moving the operation to Dagenham. Even though the line had been open in Cork only since 1929, Ford could not argue with the figures and facts. Only 31,471 tractors had been built in the four model years, hardly the mass production necessary for profitability.

About the middle of August 1932, the Fordson line at Cork was torn down and shipped to Dagenham. The new line was up and running on February 19, 1933. During the transfer, the venerable Fordson was given a facelift. This included a striking blue paint job, conventional fenders with the toolbox on the dash, a ribbed pattern cast into the radiator tank, and the Fordson name cast in the radiator side panels. The fuel tank end now said "Ford Motor Company, Ltd., Made in England."

Production got off to a slow start at Dagenham because of the Depression, with weekly production of less than seventy units through 1934.

In 1932, Franklin Delano Roosevelt was elected president by a frustrated American electorate that was tired of former-President Hoover's apparent "do-nothing" policy. Roosevelt considered his election a mandate to "do-something-even-if-wrong." His New Deal program changed the country to such an extent that the effects are still emerging sixty years later. There are many who, in retrospect, believe the New Deal had little to do with ending the US Depression, let alone worldwide problems. Rather, today it seems that it was expenditures for World War II that brought a return to prosperity.

Nevertheless, the New Deal was good for the farmers of the thirties. Just three months after Roosevelt took the oath of office, Congress passed his Agricultural Adjustment Act. In exchange for direct subsidy payments, farmers were to curtail production. Other New Deal legislation called for the distribution of farm surpluses to those "on relief," soil conservation measures, farm credit, rural electrification, and resettlement of inhabitants of uneconomical farms. Although some of these measures were later deemed unconstitutional, the farmers, and hence the farm machinery makers, began to prosper. By 1936 tractor sales were almost what they had been in 1929. And this was true for the Dagenham Fordson, as well.

In 1935, the Fordson tractor was updated with the following changes:

A 40-degree angled steering wheel; a double leaf seat spring mounted behind the axle; optional pneumatic tires; conventional fenders; vertical exhaust pipe; longer starting crank; lights; differential-mounted PTO; and orange trim on the blue paint.

This 1942 Fordson N is a Hop Garden Conversion by Invicta Motor Works, Canterbury, Kent. The wheelbase has been shortened and narrowed to enable the tractor to maneuver between the hop vines.

A 1941 Fordson N half track.

The All-Around

In 1937, the Fordson celebrated its twentieth birthday with a new model; the tricycle-configured Fordson All-Around. This was an attempt to get in on the move toward all-purpose, or general purpose, row-crop tractors that swept American farms in the thirties.

The all-purpose tractor was born out of a desire to design a tractor that could replace not just *some* of the horses, but *all* the horses on the farm. Characteristic of the tractors developed for this purpose was the tricycle configuration that did away with the low front axle. Now front-mounted cultivators were practical and a big part of the horse's domain was invaded. Another characteristic of these all-purpose machines was the placement of a power-takeoff on the rear so that pulled harvesters could be powered by the tractor's engine. The new Fordson All-Around had such a PTO.

A 1938 Fordson All-Around. The All-Around was made between 1937-1940. It was essentially the same as the standard-tread Fordson, but catered to the interest of the American farmer in row-crop tractors during that period. The All-Around could be equipped with a front-mounted cultivator.

Besides these important changes, the late 1937 model was also given a bright new orange paint job, an oil bath air cleaner, and higher compression heads for both the gas and distillate models.

Distillate, or Tractor Vaporizing Oil (TVO), was just coming on the market. It allowed the use of higher compression than did kerosene, and hence, more power was produced without increasing displacement or operating speed. Since the Fordson engine was about pushed to its limits, this high compression route to more power was tried, along with another 100rpm. Nebraska tests indicate a belt rating of 21.3hp, only slightly better than the 21.05hp achieved with the 1930 version. The Fordson's diminishing reputation was further damaged when the high-compression engines began developing bearing and oil consumption problems.

These problems were mostly overcome with the 1939 model when some head and piston redesigns were incorporated. The 1939 model, because of the onset of World War II, also saw a change to green paint. Green was the Fordson's color, except for the many military variations, until production of the Model N ended in 1945.

Thus ended a twenty-eight year production run (counting the MOMs of 1917), a record exceeded only by the John Deere Model D record of thirty years (1923-1953). Quite an accomplishment for a tractor that was dismissed by the experts of 1917 as being "too light to stand up." The Fordson was loved by some, hated by others. In its last years of being imported to the United States, its market share dropped to around 5 percent. The following widely published anonymous poem summarizes the feelings of many for the lowly Fordson:

The Fordson on the farm arose
Before the dawn at four:
It milked the cows and washed the clothes
And finished every chore.

Then forth it went into the field
Just at the break of day,
It reaped and threshed the golden yield
and hauled it all away.

It plowed the field that afternoon,
And when the job was through
It hummed a pleasant little tune
and churned the butter, too.

For while the farmer, peaceful-eyed,
Read by the tungsten's glow,
His patient Fordson stood outside
And ran the dynamo.

The years 1939-1945 were war years. In 1943, Edsel Ford died of cancer and 80-year-old Henry Ford resumed the presidency of the company. Young Henry Ford, Edsel's son then in the US Navy, soon returned to Detroit to assist in day-to-day operations. The war years also saw the rise to prominence of Harry Ferguson and his "System." In Harry Ferguson, Henry Ford found a kindred spirit. A spirit not shared by Lord Percival Perry, who wanted nothing to do with the eccentric inventor. These, however, are chronicles for the next chapter.

A 1937 blue-with-orange trim Fordson All-Around is shown here on the Zillmer farm near Algoma, Wisconsin. Note the special wheels. The inner and outer rings can be removed, leaving only the skeleton lug ring.

Collecting Comments

The Cork Fordson N; Serial No. 747682-779135

Because of their fewer numbers, Cork Fordsons are prized by collectors. Quite a number of them were sent to the United States and Canada. The Sherman Brothers, confidants of Henry Ford, were big Fordson importers and dealers. They would also play a big part in subsequent events.

Imported Cork, or Irish Fordsons as they were called, found many uses other than on the farm. There were the usual golf course, industrial, and grader conversions, some with half or full tracks.

Characteristics of the Cork Fordson N 1929-1932:
Engine: Ford-built, 4.125x5in bore and stroke, 267ci, four-cylinder, L-head, rated at 1100rpm

Weight: 3,600lb
Transmission: Three speeds forward, one reverse
Final Drive: Worm and wheel, double-lead worm
Brakes: Transmission disk brake clutch pedal-operated
Color: Light gray with bright red wheels, 7-spoke rears
Labeling: Solid-side radiator cover with "Fordson" cast on the front. "Made in Irish Free State" or "in Cork, Ireland" on tank end
Heavy front axle with downward bend in the middle
Cast front wheels
Five rounded triangular holes in the front wheel disks
Standard equipment: Tapered toolbox fenders

A pair of Fordsons grace the Zillmer farm on the shores of Lake Michigan near Algoma, Wisconsin. In the foreground is a 1937 Fordson All-Around; behind is a 1950 E27N Major.

This 1938 Fordson All-Around was equipped from the factory with rubber tires. Note the weighted front wheels. Fordsons of this period were painted orange. This one is configured for gasoline and uses the high-compression head. Thus equipped, the Fordson was rated at 30 maximum belt horsepower.

The Dagenham Fordson N 1933-1945, Regulars and All-Arounds; Serial No. 779154-980519

Only 2,807 Fordsons were produced in 1933 because of the move to Dagenham and the slowness of tractor sales due to the Great Depression. Model year 1933 Fordsons with serial numbers between 779154 and 781966 should be given an extra star.

The 1933 Fordson received a considerable facelift over the previous models, including the blue paint job. In 1935, it received another upgrade and orange trim on the blue paint. Then in 1937 production was split between All-Around and Regular versions. The paint was switched at that point to all orange. This only lasted until World War II started in 1939. Then the standard paint color became green.

Characteristics of the Dagenham Fordson N 1933-1945:
Engine: Ford-built, 4.125x5in bore and stroke, 267ci, four-cylinder, L-head, rated at 1100rpm
Weight: 4,000lb
Transmission: Three speeds forward, one reverse
Final Drive: Worm and wheel, double-lead worm.
Brakes: Transmission disk brake clutch pedal-operated
Labeling: "Fordson" on the radiator side cover and on the front. "Made in England" on the fuel tank end
Cast front wheel disks
Five rounded triangular holes in the front wheel disks
Standard equipment: Plain fenders, toolbox on dash
Pneumatic tires optional after 1935

Marlo Remme on his orange 1938 Fordson All-Around. Remme is from Dennison, Minnesota, and has had the tractor for three years. It spent most of its previous life in the Austin, Minnesota, area.

Fordson N Serial Numbers

Year	Beginning Numbers	Dagenham	Beginning Numbers
Cork		1937	807581
1929	747682	1938	826779
1930	757369	1939	837826
1931	772565	1940	854238
1932	776066	1941	874914
		1942	897624
Dagenham		1943	925274
1933	779154	1944	957574
1934	781967	1945	975419
1935	785548		
1936	794703		

Chapter 4

Ford-Ferguson

Model 9N 1939-1942
★★★★★ Serial No. 1-1000
★★★★ Serial No. 1001-45975
★★★ Serial No. 45976-88887
★★★★ Serial No. 88888-99002
For 9NAN models, add one star unless
already a 5-star

Model 2N
★★★★ Serial No. 99003-105374
★★★ Serial No. 105375-169981
★★ Serial No. 169982-290000
★★★ Serial No. 290001-296000
★★★★ Serial No. 296001 and up
For 2NAN models, add one star
For non-electrical, steel-wheel Model
2Ns, add one star

"You haven't got enough money to buy my patents," said Harry Ferguson to Henry Ford in the fall of 1938. If anyone could have bought them, Ford could, as he was probably the richest man in the world at that time.

"Well, you need me as much as I need you," responded Ford, "so what do you propose?"

"A gentleman's agreement," explained Ferguson. "You stake your reputation and resources on this idea, I stake a lifetime of design and invention—no written agreement could be worthy of what this represents. If you trust me, I'll trust you."

"It's a good idea," said Ford. The two men stood from the kitchen table and chairs brought outside for their meeting at Ford's Fair Lane estate and shook hands.

Thus, was born the most revolutionary concept in farm tractors in the twentieth century. This famous Handshake Agreement spawned the integration of tractor and implement, replacing the idea of the tractor as a puller or pusher of its tools, an idea carried over from the days of the horse.

Identified as the 9N, the Ford-Ferguson (Ford tractor, Ferguson System) incorporated a load compensating hydraulic implement lift system. Virtually every farm tractor built since the patents ran out or could be circumvented has embodied its principles. Ferguson's system, known as the three-point hitch with draft control, is still very much in evidence today.

The similarity between the Ford-Ferguson name and Fordson resulted in much confusion. Complicating matters, in 1947 Ford abrogated the Handshake Agreement and began producing the 8N Ford tractor, which looked the same. Ferguson, thwarted in the United States by the 8N and in England by the continued production of the Ford-son, launched his own look-alike tractor. Now there were Fordsons, Ford-Fergusons, Fergusons, and Fords. Many old-timers refer to them all as Fordsons.

Henry George "Harry" Ferguson

Harry Ferguson was born in 1884 on a farm in County Down, Northern Ireland. He had a penchant for confrontation with both his father and his schoolmasters. He left school at the age of 14. From then until about the age of 27, he worked on the family farm, for himself, or for his brother's automobile repair business.

During this time, he tried his hand at automobile and motorcycle racing. And in 1909 he designed, built, and flew an airplane, a monoplane; it was the first of any kind to be flown in Ireland.

Harry Ferguson was small of stature, and as a young man on the farm came to hate the struggle of horse plowing. In good conditions, a man and a team could plow two acres per day, which took all the energy of the plowman. Added to the effort of controlling the plow was the requirement to man-handle it around the headlands. In poor, rocky Irish soil, the job was much harder. It's no wonder the famous American plow maker, James Oliver, said, "The man who hasn't been jerked up astride his plow handles hasn't had his vocabulary tested!"

Ferguson and Tractors

When World War I loomed, the Irish Board of Agriculture appointed Ferguson to oversee tractor maintenance and records for all of Ireland. With

41

the internal combustion engine tractor, Ferguson saw his future. Some of the early farm engines and tractors were brought into his brother's shop for repair and Harry wondered at their size and weight. They hardly seemed practical.

By 1914 the Waterloo Boy tractor was in production. It was still quite large and heavy, but at 6,200lb it was a step in the right direction. Ferguson established a stockholder company known as Harry Ferguson, Ltd., and took on a Waterloo Boy dealership.

By now, the Model T Ford was winning the hearts and minds of people all over the world. Enterprising industrialists were capitalizing on its popularity with farmers by offering Model T-to-tractor conversion kits. One of these was the Eros conversion, manufactured in St. Paul, Minnesota. It was one of the best of scores that were offered and it became popular in England and Ireland.

With such a light vehicle for a starting point, it seemed obvious to Ferguson that the common tractor plows of the day were much too heavy for the Eros. He set about designing and building a lightweight mounted plow. Harry Ferguson, Ltd., was to manufacture it. The finished plow weighed only 220lb, about half the going rate for a two-bottom plow, and it had only half the number of parts.

The Ferguson plow featured a clever attachment to the Eros-Model T. It was hitched under the belly, forward of the rear axle. Thus the force of pulling the plow was reflected downward on all four wheels, increasing traction. It also eliminated any tendency for the tractor to rear up if the plow caught on a solid object. The plow was mounted with weight-compensating balance springs that allowed the driver to raise and lower it by means of a lever beside the seat. Even though the Eros tractor enjoyed only a short time of utilization, the Ferguson plow sold quite well.

Before several months of MOM Fordson plowing had been completed, the first driver had been killed by a rearing accident. The plow had struck a submerged rock. The cleats of the tractor were buried in the turf and could not slip. The relatively high-speed engine with its heavy flywheel drove the body of the tractor around the now stationary rear axle, pinning the driver to the ground. The Fordson became so noted for this tendency that aftermarket clutch depressors and ignition interrupters were sold for them. Finally, in 1924, Ford even offered the "tailed" fenders designed to pop the cleats out of the ground and allow slippage before the tractor went over.

Harry Ferguson might have greeted the Fordson with resentment, since it spelled the end of his Eros plow. Not one to miss opportunity, Ferguson instead saw the Fordson as providing a real plow market.

In the fall of 1917 when Charles Sorensen came to London to discuss setting up production in Cork, Ireland, Ferguson rushed to meet him, plow drawings in hand.

"Your tractor's all right as far as it goes," he told Sorensen, "but it really doesn't solve the fundamental problems."

Sorensen was somewhat put off by the remark, but Ferguson had his attention. Ferguson rolled out the Eros plow drawings for Sorensen, and using his persuasive gift, convinced him of the desirability of his under-belly line of draft.

Harry Ferguson's earnestness, enthusiasm, and confidence won over Charles Sorensen. The meeting ended with Sorensen's commitment to support development of the Ferguson plow for the new Ford tractor. Later, when the handshake deal was going sour, Sorensen regretted the commitment.

"Had I foreseen the consequences of that meeting," he later wrote, "I would have avoided it."

Draft Control

Ferguson and his design team, which by then included Willie Sands, John Williams, and Archie Greer, set about the design of their Fordson plow. To overcome the rearing tendency and to transfer draft loads to all four wheels, a duplex linkage consisting of two parallel links mounted one above the other was employed. This arrangement was rigid in the vertical plane, but allowed movement in the lateral plane for steering.

Ferguson got the Roderick Lean Company, of Mansfield, Ohio, to manufacture the Fordson plow in the United States, but in 1924, the company went bankrupt. Next, Ferguson made a manufacturing arrangement with the Sherman Brothers, George and Eber, who were Fordson distributors for the state of New York and confidants of Henry Ford. To make the plow, the firm of Ferguson-Sherman, Incorporated, was set up with a plant in Evansville, Indiana.

The Duplex Hitch plow was a success and sales were brisk. Like the Eros plow, the Fordson Duplex Hitch plow was strictly mechanical. To keep the furrow depth fairly constant, a Floating Skid device was invented. It worked well enough for the plow, but now Ferguson and his team were working on other implements such as harrows and cultivators. The researchers turned to hydraulics and added another link to the Duplex Hitch.

The reaction of draft loads worked on a hydraulic valve so that as draft load increased or decreased, the implement automatically raised or lowered in such a way as to keep the draft load constant. A plow running at 8in of depth, for example, encountered hard soil, increasing draft loads caused the plowing depth to be reduced to, say 6in, until the hard going was passed. Then the plow was automatically returned to its original depth. Also, the act of raising the plow dramatically increased the download on the rear wheels, reducing slippage. This concept was patented under the title of Draft Control.

The Black Tractor

When US Fordson production ended in 1928, Harry Ferguson realized there was no likelihood of getting his system incorporated into that tractor. Instead, he began designing a tractor from scratch with the hydraulics built in, not added on. When the drawings were finished, Ferguson began contacting companies specializing in the required parts.

The result was a diminutive Fordson-type machine weighing only a little more than half of the Fordson's weight. The engine was from Hercules, and the transmission and differential were supplied by David Brown. It was painted black, and since it had no other name, it came to be called "The Black Tractor."

Although the Black Tractor had several debilitating shortcomings, it performed well enough to entice David Brown to undertake manufacture of an improved version to be known as the Ferguson-Brown Type A. The first of the Type A tractors was ready for sale in May 1936.

Sales of the Ferguson-Brown were disappointing, as were profits. The tractor could not be made in large enough quantities to bring the costs down, and the price was already too high, especially considering the fact that all new implements were needed. The tractor itself also had some weaknesses; in David Brown's eyes, it was just too small. Brown and Ferguson eventually had a falling out, and Brown began making the changes he thought necessary on his own.

With that, Harry Ferguson contacted his friends the Sherman Brothers. Could they get him an audience with Henry Ford for a demonstration of his tractor, he asked? They could, and did.

The Handshake Agreement

In the fall of 1938, Ferguson and several aides brought a crated Ferguson-Brown tractor and implements by ship and truck to Ford's Fair Lane Estate. Ford had several associates with him there, and all assembled agreed the Ferguson-Brown handily outperformed both a Fordson and an Allis Chalmers with the same-size plow.

Ford took on a serious attitude and called for a table and chairs to be brought out of the estate's kitchen. Ford and Ferguson seated themselves at the table and Ferguson proceeded to demonstrate the function of the system by using a spring-wound model. The result of this conversation was a handshake, sealing a gentleman's agreement that Ford would build the tractors incorporating Ferguson's Draft Control hydraulic system. Ferguson was to set up dealerships and have implements built. Further, it was agreed that either could terminate the agreement at will and without explanation. Ford must have been really impressed by Harry Ferguson and his demonstrations as he not only agreed to the deal (which held a much greater profit potential for Ferguson), he also agreed to loan Ferguson $50,000 to get his operation started.

Development of the Model 9N

The new tractor was designated the 9N: 9 for the year 1939; N the Ford designation for tractor. It was a vast improvement over both the Fordson and the Ferguson-Brown. It retained the unified frameless structure of its predecessors, but used what has become known as the "utility tractor front axle." This is a straight axle pivoted in the

Dwight Emstrom's 9N Serial number 356 has its aluminum hood unpainted and polished to shine like chrome. Those who are lucky enough to find tractors with these cast hoods often do the same, just to prove that they really are aluminum. The chain loop below the grille is used to tie the tractor down to Emstrom's flatbed trailer.

43

The cast, chrome-plated radiator cap used on early 9Ns. Painted cast caps were used in the war years prior to the advent of pressurized radiators. Pressure caps were stamped, rather than cast.

center and with downward-extending kingpins. With this arrangement, more crop clearance is obtained and the tractor is given a higher roll center for greater stability.

Henry Ford's main objective was that of low cost. Early on he established a goal of a selling price of less than $600, believing such a price to the farmer would result in sufficient demand to meet his production goal of 1,000 units per week. That would be enough to keep an assembly line busy. To meet the cost objective, many parts from the car and truck lines were adapted:

• One-half of the Mercury/Ford truck 239ci V-8 was used. This included pistons, rings, valves, rods, pins, some gaskets, and bearings. The V-8 was rated at 95hp at 3600rpm; the tractor engine, however, would be rated at a conservative 1400rpm to start with, but its governor would al-

Even though Ferguson sold the tractors to the public, Ford did some advertising on its own. Here the pitch is that the Ford-Ferguson tractor is a way to keep boys on the farm. The rather hokey picture is from the press introduction of June 1939. The boy on the left is the 8-year-old who gave the plowing demonstration. The boy on the right appears to have been added to the picture later.

Your Post-War Tractor should...

AUTOMATICALLY CHANGE its "WEIGHT" to SUIT the JOB

Only the FORD TRACTOR with FERGUSON SYSTEM gives you this ECONOMY—*today*

WHEN YOU THINK about your tractor of the future, you have a right to expect that it will give you freedom from guessing how much weight to pile on to pull through those tough spots on your farm. And freedom from straining your back, skinning your knuckles and barking your shins putting cumbersome steel or concrete wheel weights into place.

It also should be unnecessary for you to pay for the hundreds of pounds of dead metal built into ordinary tractors of today, plus the fuel to carry it around, merely to provide enough traction to do an ordinary day's work.

These things you have a right to expect— why? Because the Ford Tractor with Ferguson System gives them to you today. It is the only tractor which automatically changes its "weight" to suit the job.

Downward pressure exerted on the tractor through the patented and exclusive Ferguson System replaces the excess built-in weight and added wheel weights necessary to other tractors.

As the two bottom links pull, the upper link is pushed forward and downward by the effort of the implement to tip in the direction of pull.

When the draft gets heavier, so does the downward pressure through the top link, and the tractor automatically provides itself with extra traction to do the job.

Thus, the Ford Tractor with Ferguson System gives you an amazing degree of economy no other tractor can offer—a light tractor for light work and a "heavier" tractor when more traction is needed.

This is only one of the many patented and exclusive features of this revolutionary tractor. The next time you drive by your Ford-Ferguson Dealer, stop in. He will show you all the reasons why this advanced farming machine drives crop production costs to an all-time new low level.

HARRY FERGUSON, INC.
Dearborn, Michigan

Ford Tractor

FERGUSON SYSTEM

A light tractor for economy, but one that can do heavy work without adding weights is the focus of this Ferguson ad. The fact that draft loads, with the Ferguson System, bear down on the rear wheels is the reason.

This Ferguson Duplex Hitch plow looks very much like later three-point plows. Ferguson developed the plow for the Fordson around 1920. It weighed about half as much as conventional pull-type plows and its dual connecting arrangement prevented rearing, which was a problem with the Fordson.

low operation to 2200rpm. At 2200rpm, 28hp was produced at the PTO. This same engine was later used in Ford light trucks rated at 30hp, and in the original Ford Jeep at 45hp.

• An automotive electrical system was used with a coil-type ignition system. The starter and generator were customized for the tractor, but a car battery was used.

• A car clutch with modifications was used.

• Car front wheel bearings were used.

• Truck differential gears were used.

• Truck brakes with modifications were used.

Styling, which was becoming a big thing for tractors in 1939, was assigned to the Ford styling department. The result of their efforts was an absolutely perfect blending of art deco flair with practicality and ease of production. The styling was so good that Ford changed it only a little for the next thirteen years. Competitors, when they came out with their utility tractor models, copied the essence of Ford's styling, as did Ferguson with his TE and TO models.

Despite the cost constraints, operator safety concerns dictated that fenders be standard equipment, as was the self-starter. On the other hand, running boards were not included as standard until the 8N appeared in 1947. Lights were always optional, but a PTO and reverse-flow muffler were standard.

Almost all domestic 9Ns were made to run on gasoline only, but a variation, the 9NAN was offered that used distillate. Most 9NANs were exported, many finding their way to Great Britain.

The 9NAN was fitted with a Holley Vaporizer of the same type used on the Fordson F.

Ferguson set up a new marketing company that included the Sherman Brothers called Ferguson-Sherman Manufacturing Corporation. The company was to design and build a line of implements, as well; but as the debut of the tractor neared, only a middle-buster and a cultivator were ready. The Ford design team swung into action and designed a 2-bottom plow (shaped by the carbody group copying an Oliver-Fordson plow), a planter (a copy of a Covington), and a disc harrow.

Press Introduction

In early June 1939, there was a demonstration of the 9N and its implements to the new Ferguson-Sherman dealer organization. On June 29, 1939, another much bigger affair organized in typical Harry Ferguson fashion took place with 500 invited guests. The guest list included journalists from all over the world and agricultural dignitaries. Tents were set up and lunch was served. Henry Ford, Harry Ferguson, and others, including 8-year-old David Mclaren (a Greenfield Village schoolboy), gave plowing demonstrations. The press was overwhelmed when young David's furrows were just as even as those run by the experienced plowmen. Both Henry and Harry admitted that they might still be on the farm if they had had a 9N when they were 8 years old. (Ford once commented, "I have walked many a weary mile behind a plow, and I know the drudgery of it.")

"It was a bad day for old Dobbin," said the opening line of the *Chicago Journal of Commerce* in its coverage of the 9N demonstration. Indeed, there were still 17 million horses at work on farms in North America in 1939. They were the targeted competition of the Ford and Ferguson design team, not the myriad of other tractors offered for sale in that era.

Production

The 9N was in production for six months in 1939 (actually the model year ended in November). Despite normal introduction problems with the assembly line and with the supply of subcontractor parts, over 10,000 Ford-Fergusons were sold yet that year. The launch price was $585 including rubber tires, an electrical system with starter, fenders, PTO, oil-bath air cleaner, oil filter, and an automobile-type reverse flow muffler (which made the tractor "quiet as a dragonfly").

Besides the three-point hitch system, the Ferguson team contributed an ingenious front wheel tread adjusting system. The front axle consisted of an angled center section that overlapped two outboard stub sections to which the wheels attached. Radius rods held the axle in place, a practice typical of Ford cars in those days. Steering linkages ran parallel to the radius rods down both sides of the tractor. The axle sections were provided with a series of holes and two bolts for each side. Axle length could be readily changed by changing the amount of overlap. Each side could be done independent of the other side, and no adjustment of steering linkage was required, due to the cleaver geometry of the Ferguson patent. Rear wheel tread could be changed by changing the position of the wheels on the wheel discs or by reversing the discs.

The tractor was an immediate success. Even with the requirement to buy all new implements, it was still cheaper than tractors that had its work capability. It took a John Deere Model G to equal the 9Ns acre per hour plowing rate, and a 1939 John Deere G cost more than twice the Ford's $585. There was some resistance to the 9N's rear-mounted cultivator, and indeed most farmers with serious cultivating to do opted for the row-crop tractor and front cultivator. Today, however, almost all cultivation is done by rear units following exactly the Ferguson concept.

The only weakness that the 9N couldn't deny was the fact that it was too light to do much serious work without the weight-transferring aid of the three-point implements. Thus the 9N made a poor showing at its first Nebraska Test (Test Number 339). Not understanding the common practice of weighting test tractors for all they were worth, Ford sent the 9N with only 300lb of calcium chloride for ballast. To keep wheel-spin down, they called for a drawbar rating engine speed of only 1400rpm. Thus, the data show the 9N developing only 12.8 drawbar horsepower. The belt tests were done at 2000rpm and produced a respectable 23.07hp.

World War II

When World War II began in December 1941, much of American industry was already gearing up for war production. Restrictions were immediately placed on strategic materials such as chromium and copper. "Civilian" automobile and light truck production was halted in February of the 1942 model year. The War Production Board issued quotas for the manufacture of heavy trucks and tractors.

By changing the model designation of the 9N to 2N (for 1942), and by eliminating starters, generators, and rubber tires, Ford was able to get more tractors into its quota. The designation change also allowed Ferguson to get a price increase past the Price Board.

Thus the 2N came to be. Before the year was out, the restricted items began reappearing on the tractor, and by 1943, most had electrics and rubber tires.

Ferguson's Difficulties

Farm Implement News of July 13, 1939, commented that the new Ford-Ferguson tractor was a triumph for Harry Ferguson, "for it put a seal of approval on a man who's been telling the same story to all and sundry, the wide world over, and they largely looked and passed on. And he has

The Ferguson Duplex Hitch plow attached to a 1926 Fordson (note the tapered fender tails). The plow is coupled to the Fordson by two clevises, one above the other. A patented "Floating Skid" controlled depth. Raising the plow was done by the hand lever and the counterbalance spring.

been doing this for about 20 years!"

Harry Ferguson, after years of struggle to extricate himself from his humble beginnings, had now hit the big time. Bearing in mind that he was regularly referred to as a "cocky Irishman" even before success, one can see that this cognomen could be upgraded to "insufferable Irishman" after success.

Henry Ford seemed at all times to regard Ferguson with great respect, even comparing his genius to that of Thomas Edison, Ford's idol. It would seem, in retrospect, that Ford had assured Ferguson that the 9N would replace the Fordson on the Dagenham assembly line and that Ferguson would be given a seat on the board of directors of Ford Motor Company (England) Ltd.

In September 1939, Harry Ferguson left the US operations in the hands of the Sherman Brothers and returned to England. Lord Percival Perry, Chairman of Ford Motor Company (England), Ltd., was not about to get involved with the feisty commoner, who had the reputation of demanding his own way. Besides, England was now at war and the government was dictating the expenditure of resources. Any change to the current-production Fordson was out of the question. Ferguson reluctantly decided to bide his time until the end of the war.

Next, Ferguson had a falling out with the Shermans that eventually resulted in a split. A new company, Harry Ferguson, Incorporated, was established to handle distribution of tractors and implements.

In 1943, Edsel Ford died of cancer and Henry, the 80-year-old automobile pioneer was pressed back into the daily running of his company. Young Henry Ford II, his grandson, returned

Some characteristics of the early 9Ns are shown here. The four-spoke steering wheel was used throughout the 9N's life and was identical to that used on Ford trucks (except for the horn button). Notice the starter button and key protruding from the panel. The safety interlock starter and steering column key appeared in mid-1940. There is also a red "Ignition-on" light just below the ammeter. Also note that there is no latch knob for the fuel-battery door. The first 9Ns (1939 models) used a completely removable snap-in cover rather than the hinged cover used after 1940. The dashboard, steering post, and transmission cover were cast aluminum, as was the grille and some hoods on 1939 models.

The unique original "hat-section" rims are shown here just outside the attach bolts. Note the smooth hubs characteristic of 1939 models.

from the Navy to help guide the corporation. The stress proved too much for the elder Ford, who suffered a series of partially debilitating strokes, finally succumbing to death in 1947 at the age of 83. Young Henry was able to get his grandfather to hand over control of the company to him in 1945 and he became the company's third president. Young Henry was thus able to wrest control away from Harry Bennett, one of Old Henry's confidants and a one-time bouncer and strong man Ford had hired to thwart the onset of the labor unions in the twenties.

Before the death of Henry Ford, Ferguson had written him complaining about his impasse with Ford, UK, and stating that he would be setting up a manufacturing facility in England to manufacture his own 9N-type tractor. A Ford aide wisely filed the letter without showing it to the elder Mr. Ford.

New Management

When Henry Ford II took over the company in 1945, he found he had an onerous task to get things back in order. The effects of his grandfather's inattention, Harry Bennett's ineptness, and the changes wrought by World War II production had left the company foundering.

Being only 28 years old at the time, Young Ford enlisted the aid of the brightest business heads obtainable, a group of other young managers and executives who became known as the "Whiz Kids." Probably the most famous of these is Robert McNamara, who later became Secretary of Defense in the Kennedy/Johnson years. It didn't take the Whiz Kids and Henry Ford II long to see that making tractors for another company to sell did not make much business sense, especially when they were being sold at a loss. This management team cared little about Old Henry's altruistic statement to the press, back in 1939, that he didn't care to make a profit on the tractor. "I'm going the limit to help my country," Henry Ford had said.

The idea of basing a project of this magnitude on a verbal agreement seemed to the new management as bad business judgment, which, in light of the fact that one of the parties had died, it probably was. One thing seemed clear, there was the understanding that either side could terminate the agreement without explanation. Therefore, in mid-1946, Henry Ford II told Harry Ferguson that the agreement would end in one year. Ford then set his engineers to building an improved version, which would be identified as the 8N (for the year 1948). He also set up a separate firm, Dearborn Motors, to do what Ferguson had been doing.

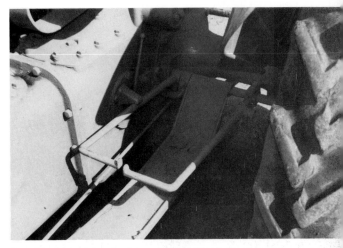

Another identifying feature of 1939 9Ns is the identical left and right brake pedals.

The Lawsuit

By this time, Ferguson was building his TE-20 in Coventry, England. It was a dead ringer in looks to the 9N-2N, but had some worthwhile improvements (such as a four-speed transmission). With Ford's withdrawal from the Handshake Agreement, Ferguson was forced to import TE-20s

This 1940 9N has the safety starter, but has the key in the second dash-mounted position, indicating a midyear production. Earlier 1940 models had the key on the right side of the dash. The key was moved to the steering post for the 1941 model. The dark spot below the ammeter is the "Ignition-on" light. This red warning light generally disappeared when the tractors became equipped with the safety starter. Obviously, there was some overlap. Dwight Emstrom owns this tractor, serial number 120886.

The 1941 9N had a unique solid grille center bar. This example also has original bulb-type non-sealed beam headlights.

to supply his dealers and to utilize the implement production he had going. Ferguson also immediately launched a project to establish a US version, the TO-20, to be made in Detroit. What really piqued Harry Ferguson, however, was that Ford was continuing to use the three-point system, almost without change. On January 8, 1948, Ferguson brought suit against Ford, in the amount of $251 million, for loss of business and for the unlicensed use of the Ferguson System, which was patented, on the 8N tractor.

After long and costly proceedings, Harry Ferguson settled out of court for $9,250,000. This was only to cover unauthorized use of Ferguson's hydraulic system. The claim for loss of business was dismissed; the success of Ferguson's TO-20 belied any damages. Ford was instructed to stop building the 8N in 1952, but by then Ferguson's patents were running out. Most modern tractors therefore have three-point hitches with some form of draft control, thanks to the pioneering efforts of Harry Ferguson.

Collecting Comments

Model 9N and 2N tractors are very collectible just because of their age. Naturally, the older they are, the higher the star rating, but with exceptions. Kerosene-burners, and 2Ns originally on steel and with the magneto ignition, rate an extra star. Early and late 2Ns rate higher than some 9Ns because of the desirability to the collector of these serial numbers.

Originality of all parts and details are essen-

tial to realize the investment potential. Details such as original "Ford" and "Ferguson System" badges are rare, as are original rear rims, especially in the 32in size. Modern tread tires detract from the value of the tractor as an antique. At least find some 45 degree tread tires, if you are not so lucky as to come up with 8.00x32 tires with the "Ford" script on them (as some have done).

Finally, the Ford-Ferguson was a system tractor. To have realized its full potential when it was new, you needed matching implements. To reach its full potential as an antique, it also needs a correct-period implement. While a common Ferguson 2-bottom plow is fine, something out of the ordinary like a Ferguson 2-way plow, or a Ferguson side mower really sets it off.

Model 9N 1939-1942

Just three months after the Handshake Agreement, experimental models of the 9N were ready for testing. Another six months saw completion of the prototype, which incorporated all the important features and the styled sheet metal.

Ferguson induced Henry Ford to put his name on a Ferguson System badge along with the familiar Ford oval. Many in Ford's management were against this, including Edsel Ford (who was then president), but on the advice of the Ford patent council, Ferguson's demand for recognition was satisfied. Some old reports indicate Ferguson even wanted top billing.

In June 1939, the first production models came off the line. Because of the short development time, the production engineering was done simultaneously with the design work. When it became obvious that steel stamping equipment would not be ready in time to support production, Sorensen had forms made and cast the hoods from aluminum. Thus the first 700 to 800 tractors came off the line with cast aluminum hoods. Other critical parts were also made of cast aluminum, some of which continued through the 1940 model. One report indicates that Sorensen's son had an aluminum foundry, and that Sorensen sent business his way both for expediency and to give him some solid production business. Besides the hoods, early 9Ns have cast aluminum dash panels and steering columns, transmission covers, and battery carriers.

Characteristics of the Model 9N:
Engine: Ford-built, 3.187x3.75in bore and stroke, 119.7ci, four-cylinder, L-head, rated at 2000rpm. Novi flyball governor capable of governing to 2200rpm. Pressurized lubrication system with full-flow cartridge-type filter. Water pump cooling. Compression ratio 6:1 (gaso-

A unique original 1942 2N. War-time restrictions on civilian production caused Ford to make these tractors without starters, generators, or rubber tires. Later, as material restrictions eased, 2Ns be- came much like the earlier 9Ns. In fact, parts books do not differentiate between 9Ns and 2Ns. This example is owned by Palmer Fossum.

The subtle differences between the original 9N (above) and 2N "Ferguson System" badges are shown in this picture.

The valuable "hat-section" rear rim is shown here on a 2N. Because of their construction, these rims trapped leaking sodium chloride tire fluid and rust set in. Good hat-section rims are now difficult to find, but are necessary for a proper restoration job. Note the exposed fender-attach bolt that is charac- teristic of 2N and up models.

51

line); 4.75:1 for 9NAN which resulted in less horsepower

Weight: 2,340lb, early; 2475lb, late

Transmission: Three speeds forward, one reverse

Final Drive: Spiral bevel gear drive with straddle-mounted pinion, 6.66:1 ratio

Brakes: Independent brakes on each rear wheel controlled by pedals on each side of the tractor; no means to lock pedals together. When the clutch pedal is fully depressed, an interconnect link applies the left brake. Thus, by using both feet, both brakes can be applied for straight-line stopping.

Standard equipment: Fenders; toolbox on left side under hood; pneumatic tires (front: 4.00x19;

These interesting casting numbers on the front of a Ford-Ferguson's rear axle give the date 12-8-45 (upside down). The casting number above (right side up) indicates it is for a 2N.

This is the pent-roof type radiator used on 9N tractors. Later tractors, with pressurized radiators, had rounded upper tanks.

rear, 8x32, early, 10x28 late)

Hydraulic Implement Control: A four-cylinder scotch yoke pump supplies pressure to a rockshaft ram. The pressure flow is controlled by a servo valve. The position of the valve handle corresponds to the position of the implement. There is therefore no "neutral" position, as is the case with other systems. The valve is also controlled by the draft linkage which effects the patented Draft Control. The valve functions to cut off flow to the supply side of the pump, rather than the pressure side, as is common.

Paint: Machine gray (to save costs, the same paint was used as that used on factory machinery)

Year-by-Year Changes
Original 1939 model features:
• Aluminum hood and side panels—first 700 to 800

- Key and starter button on the dash
- An "Ignition-On" light on the dash
- Grease fittings on the front of the kingpin housings
- 2-ribbed fenders, bolted/riveted to brackets
- 4-spoked steering wheel
- Smooth rear axle hubs
- Front axle radius rods are I-beam type
- 4-bladed pusher fan
- No freeze plugs on side of engine block
- Very square exhaust manifold cross-section
- The battery/fuel tank filler cover is a snap-in (not hinged)
- Grille is cast aluminum with semi-horizontal spokes
- Left and right brake pedals are interchangeable
- Extensive use of aluminum castings for: dash and steering housing, battery stand, lift quadrant, and transmission cover and inspection plates

Changes introduced in 1940
- Safety Starter introduced midyear
- Key is first on the right side of dash, then on the left side
- A hinged battery cover replaces the snap-in at midyear
- The 3-brush generator becomes standard
- Fenders with single ribs are introduced midyear
- Freeze plugs appear in sides of engine block
- Some steel castings replace aluminum
- Exhaust manifold becomes more rounded in cross section

Changes for 1941
- Left and right brake pedals are now different
- Kingpin grease fittings are moved to the rear
- A steel grille with vertical bars and solid center is used
- A three-spoke steering wheel is introduced midyear with covered, or solid, spokes
- There is liberal use of chrome trim
- The hubs are now riveted, rather than smooth
- Heavier duty lift cylinder and spring
- Key is moved to the steering column
- 6-blade fan replaces 4-blade (can be pusher or puller)
- Aluminum dash castings now steel
- Lube provided to governor by line from oil filter

Changes for 1942
1942 Model 9Ns are mostly like the 1941 model. As parts were used up, 2N characteristics appeared.

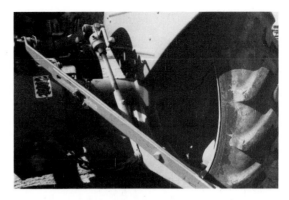

Note the solid fender-bolt receptacle built into the rear axle of this 9N. Model 2N and up used a receptacle with an open space in the center.

Model 2N

After producing 99,002 9Ns in about thirty-two months, the model designation was changed to 2N. There had been a continuous series of changes to the 9N as it matured, but the designation was not changed. With the beginning of World War II, War Production Board restrictions limited the use of copper and rubber for non-military applications. Production of tractors was curtailed, but each manufacturer was allowed a percentage of their former production.

The redesignated tractor, the 2N, was there-

The 7 in the casting mark on the flywheel housing of 2N Ford-Fergusons indicates that it is a 1947 model.

The last digit of flywheel housing casting marks indicate the year model of most 2Ns. Shown are 1944 and 1946 models.

This 1941 Ford-Ferguson has a mounted Fergu-son mower. Characteristics of later 9Ns are shown on this tractor: single ribbed fenders, riveted axle hub, and hinged battery cover.

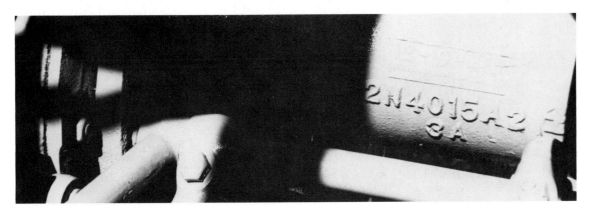

Casting numbers and dates that appeared in 1945 on rear axles are shown here. Although hard to read, the date above the 2N number is 12-9-46.

fore made without an electrical system (saving the copper from the starter and generator) and without rubber tires. A magneto ignition system was substituted for the coil-type. Steel and aluminum were substituted for copper (brass) in the radiator, as well. In addition, as part of the wartime restrictions, all brightmetal was replaced with black trim paint.

Before the year 1942 was out, the material restrictions were eased and production quotas relaxed. The Model 2N received its starter, generator, and rubber tires. Production continued to mid-1947, with annual and midyear changes occurring as they did on the 9N.

Characteristics of the Model 2N and Year-by-Year Changes:

There are no fundamental differences between the 9N and the 2N except those shown following as year-by-year changes. Parts books list the two models together, and though the two are not necessarily the same, 9N and 2N parts are generally interchangeable, except for early and late transmission gears.

Changes introduced for 1942
- A slotted grille center bar appears
- The steering wheel now has three spokes with rod spokes
- 10.00x28 tires become standard, 8.00x32 optional
- Valve rotators are used
- A non-electrical, steel-wheeled version produced

The Ferguson mounted mower in the down position. The position of the mower could be controlled by the three-point quadrant even while the mower was in operation.

Pulleys, cables, levers, springs, and cranks are
needed for operation of this Ferguson mower.

More details of the operating mechanism of the
Ferguson mower mounted on the 1941 9N. The
three-point hitch has been disabled and blocked in
position. One lift arm has been removed while the
other has a special cable-puller arm installed. Raising this arm hydraulically raises the mower. The
mower is driven by the double V-belt pulley set.

The 1941 Ford-Ferguson with the Ferguson mower. Here, the mower is shown in the transport position. Note the mower bracket and linkage on the tractor's left side below the toolbox. Most three-point mowers are mounted behind the rear wheels and are inconvenient for the operator to observe. Ferguson put this one out front where the operator could raise and lower it as required for jobs like highway ditch mowing. Dwight Emstrom owns this nicely restored outfit.

A 1945 2N Ford-Ferguson in what would be called "fairly straight" condition. Note that it has a replacement rim on the left rear and that there is no auxiliary transmission. Its owner had it for sale for $1,750.

Two very early 9Ns from the Palmer Fossum collection appear side by side, showing to good advantage their art deco styling. Note the smooth rear axle hubs and 8x32 rear tires.

- External fasteners appear in lower side panels at midyear
- Chrome trim is replaced by black paint
- Fender bolt holes in rear axle no longer solid, starting at midyear
- "2N" appears on lower edge of oval Ford badge

Changes for 1943
- The radiator becomes pressurized at S/N 109502
- 9.00x32 tires optional, 8.00x32 not offered

Changes for 1944
- Oval radius rods introduced midyear
- Sealed beam headlights available

- Helical transmission gears introduced midyear; case is labeled "HX"
- Identifying year number appears on flywheel housing

Changes for 1945
- Heavier rear axle housings introduced midyear
- Rear axle castings have date

Changes for 1946
- Still heavier rear axle housings used

No Changes for 1947

This 1944 2N is owned by Russell Hanson of Ellison Bay in Wisconsin's Door County peninsula. It is carrying a nice, heavy Dearborn Implements blade.

The original 9Ns weighed in at just over 2,300lb, and especially with the 8x32 rear tires, traction without the aid of the Ferguson System was lacking. Therefore, for the first Nebraska tests, the tractor was rated at only 1400rpm to prevent excessive slippage during the drawbar tests. Later, Ford engineers realized that ballasting was allowed, and full performance capabilities were demonstrated.

Serial Numbers

There is some disagreement among published serial number data. The following agrees with Ford-supplied data and with that of several other authorities. All 9Ns and 2Ns have serial numbers beginning with 9N. Tractors with a "star" after the serial number have thin-wall cylinder sleeves.

Year	Serial Numbers
9N	
1939	1
1940	10234
1941	45976
1942	88888

Year	Serial Numbers
2N	
1942	99003
1943	105375
1944	126538
1945	169982
1946	198731
1947	258504

Best guesses are that there were 197,129 2Ns made. Therefore, the last serial number would be 296131.

Note the grease fitting on the hubcap. Informed guesses say this was a one-of-a-kind method of greasing the wheel bearing. Others think it may have been a production variation. Either way, the fitting was so vulnerable to damage, it's no wonder more are not seen. This is Dwight Emstrom's 1940 9N.

The 1944 Ford-Ferguson tractor was originally a 2NAN. It's been converted to a Perkins P3 diesel by Englishman Brian Chester.

Seventy-two-year-old Russell Hanson of Ellison Bay, Wisconsin, with his 1941 Ford-Ferguson 9N, serial number 60454. Hanson has seven Ford Ns at the present time.

Dwight Emstrom's 1942 Model 2N with an early
Ferguson grader blade.

Details of the Ferguson grader blade are shown
here. These implements, and other blades either
by Ford, Ferguson, or aftermarket sources, are
among the most useful three-point tools.

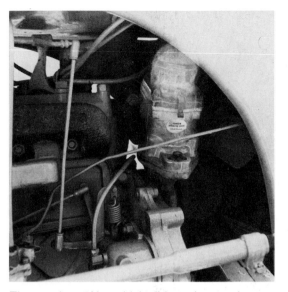

The wartime 2Ns, which did not have a battery electrical system, had a magneto ignition system. The magneto, shown here behind the fan, was driven from the regular distributor pad.

The "Armstrong" starter of the 1942 2N is clearly shown here. The 2N was fairly easy to start with the crank. It also did quite well with steel wheels, thanks to the weight transferring effect of the Ferguson three-point hitch. Nevertheless, most farmers couldn't wait to get rubber tires on their wartime 2Ns.

A late 1940 Ford-Ferguson 9N with a Ferguson dirt scoop. Note that the fenders have single ribs.

This one is owned by Dwight Emstrom of Galesburg, Illinois.

The 1940 9N retained the aluminum grille with semi-horizontal spokes of the original 1939 model. Because of the fragile nature of cast aluminum, most have since been replaced with the later steel type.

Dwight Emstrom's pristine 1946 2N with a side-mount Ferguson disc terracer and cab.

Bob Johnson restored this B-NO-40 heavy duty aircraft tug. Called the Moto-Tug, it was a conversion of a 2N made by Harry Ferguson, Incorporated, during World War II. *Bob Johnson*

Ford-Fergusons made in 1939 and some made in 1940 have the front spindle lubrication fitting on the front of the spindle as shown here; on later models it was on the back.

This 1941 9N Ford-Ferguson shows off its unique solid center bar grille. Previous 9Ns used the aluminum grille with horizontal bars. After 1941, the grille was similar to this, but had a slotted center bar.

This picture of serial number 356 Ford-Ferguson shows many of the characteristics of the early tractors. Note the 8.00x32 rear tires, Ford brand, and the single-ribbed fronts. Note also the double fender ribs and smooth rear axle hubs. Owned by Dwight Emstrom, this tractor has the cast aluminum hood and side panels.

Looking somewhat like a scale model Fordson, this 1936 Ferguson-Brown was the forerunner of the 9N Ford-Ferguson. This joint venture by Ferguson and David Brown put David Brown in the tractor business. Their tractor was the first to embody Ferguson's hydraulic 3-point hitch. When Ferguson and Brown could not agree on a marketing strategy, Ferguson pulled out of the relationship and demonstrated the Ferguson-Brown tractor to Henry Ford. The result was the famous handshake agreement and the Ford-Ferguson tractor. David Brown, left on his own, went on to build a creditable line of tractors.

Chapter 5

Modern Fordsons

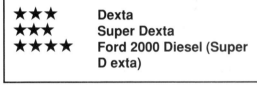

★★★	Standard
★★	Row crop
★★	Land Utility
★★★	Industrial

Add one star for the Perkins diesel engine, and add an additional star for the first and last 100 serial numbers

★★	New Fordson Major (TVO or gasoline)
★★	New Fordson Major Diesel
★	Fordson Power Major
★★	Fordson Super Major
★★★	Ford 5000 Super Major
★★	New Performance Fordson Super Major

Add one star for the first and last 100 serial numbers.

★★★	Dexta
★★★	Super Dexta
★★★★	Ford 2000 Diesel (Super D exta)

When the Allied victory in Europe seemed assured, thoughts at both the War Agricultural Committee and at Ford Motor Company, Ltd., turned to those of a new tractor. The highly successful Ford-Ferguson would have been the logical choice. Ford-Fergusons had been imported to the United Kingdom under the Lend-Lease arrangement, along with the custom Ferguson implements. The little gray tractors had comported themselves very well, especially when compared to the rather crude offerings of other manufacturers.

Several factors militated against such logic, however, not the least of which was the personality conflict between Lord Perry and other members of the board of Ford, UK, and Harry Ferguson.

The conflicts began as early as 1939, when Ferguson arrived in the United Kingdom with a Ford-Ferguson and implements and began giving demonstrations. Although audiences were mainly government officials and agricultural college professors, the real target of these demonstrations was the management of Ford Motor Company, Ltd. Unknown to Harry Ferguson at the time, Patrick Hennessey, Ford's British General Manager, had already convinced the government in 1938 to build up a stock of Fordsons against the eventuality of war. If war didn't come, Ford would sell the Fordsons to farmers while curtailing current production. Thus, neither the British government, nor Ford Motor Company, Ltd., was in a position to entertain a production switch.

When it became obvious to Ferguson that, with the war, his efforts to effect a change were going nowhere, he returned to America. The turmoil at Ford during the last war years and his complete inability to crack the British Ford Board of Directors, left Harry Ferguson with no choice but to start producing his own version of the tractor.

Note the frosted "shade" on the top part of the original headlight lens on this E27N Fordson. This 1950 model, serial number 1142487, is owned by Doug Zillmer of Algoma, Wisconsin.

Doug Zillmer's 1950 E27N Fordson Major has many of the characteristics of the Fordson N, including the engine. Measures taken to give the E27N more crop clearance are obvious in this picture. The car behind is a nice original 1931 Model A Ford.

The plan by the British government and Ford, UK, to build 3,000 Fordsons and stock them at various dealerships for later wartime use was so successful that it gave considerable pride to both Ford and the Ministry of Agriculture. This, too, contributed to the resistance to Ferguson's idea to switch to the new tractor design.

The Model E27N

At the end of hostilities in 1945, the requirements of a new tractor were established. Although production of about 150,000 Fordson Model Ns during the six wartime years had nearly worn out the production facilities, neither the time nor the material was available for a completely new design. Therefore, a complete upgrade and modernization of the venerable Fordson was undertaken.

Row-crop tractors were never as popular in the United Kingdom as they had been in America, but there was a need for more crop clearance than that provided by the Fordson. The new version would have to be higher. The War Agricultural Committee also dictated three-plow capability.

The Fordson Major Model E27N was made between 1945-1952. It used the same 267ci engine that was used in the Fordson N. Some 23,000 of the later ones were fitted with the Perkins diesel, however. The rear tires are 11.00x36 and are labeled "India Farm Tractor."

This 1950 Fordson High Major E27N is fitted with a P6 Perkins diesel and a foul weather cab.

Since the original worm-drive would not take the additional load, a redesigned rear axle with a spiral bevel drive and bull-gears was incorporated. The new rear axle, combined with a downward-extending kingpin front axle, gave the new E27N the desired higher stance. The higher tractor would no longer fit through the paint booth, so E27Ns were, at least at first, painted by hand, reverting at the same time to the blue and orange scheme of 1938.

The E in E27N was for English; 27 indicated the horsepower; and N was the Ford designator for tractors.

The almost thirty-year-old engine design was retained. The old engine's life was barely adequate, especially the high-compression gasoline (petrol) version. Worse, overhaul was an in-shop project, since the cylinders did not have sleeves and the main bearings were of the babbitt type. To keep the E27N viable, an engine exchange program was developed.

Then Frank Perkins, of Perkins Diesel, converted a Fordson for his own use to one of his diesel engines. When Ford heard of it, they sent two more Fordsons to Perkins for conversion. The result was the P6 (TA) Fordson, of which some

A Fordson E27N works a plow at The Great Dorset Steam Fair in 1993.

23,000 were built before production of the type ended in 1952.

Collecting Comments

Besides the spark-ignition and diesel engines, there were also fixed and variable front axle versions. Rubber tires were available almost from the start. There were industrial versions, and crawlers developed in association with County and Roadless. While many E27Ns were built, not many found their way to America.

Characteristics of the Model E27N:
Engine: Ford-built: 4.125x5.00in bore and stroke, 267ci, four-cylinder, L-head, rated at 1200rpm. Governor of the type used on the N. Splash lubrication system. Water pump cooling.
Perkins Diesel: 45hp at 1500rpm
Weight: 4,000lb (gas), 4,510lb (diesel)

Transmission: Three speeds forward, one reverse
Final Drive: Spiral bevel pinion with individual bull gears. Tractors from Serial Number 1141433 had stronger rear axle shafts to take the increased power of the diesel engine
Brakes: Independent brakes on each rear wheel of the Row-crop and Land Utility versions. A transmission brake of the type used on the Fordson F and N models, actuated by the clutch, was used on all E27Ns.
Standard equipment: Fenders (mudguards), several styles used
Toolbox originally on dash. Next, on Land Utility model, it was under the seat. This location interfered with the hydraulic lifts, so a left-side engine block location was used thereafter.
Pneumatic tires standard equipment on the Land Utility model, common on others (front, 6.00x19; rear, 9.00x36; 11.00x36 after 1947)

This 1950 Fordson Industrial E27N P6 was purchased new by the City of Leeds, England, street cleaning department. It has been restored to original shape by P.M. and M.P. Dean, father and son, of Galphay, North Yorkshire.

Hydraulics: Two types were used, Smith and Varley. The Smith lift used one control lever, the Varley used two. The three-point linkage was originally connected to the lift arms by chains; later solid links were used with a leveler. The Hydraulic Power Lift (HPL) was available after early 1948. The system did not provide draft control.

Paint: Dark blue with orange wheels and trim

Steering: Model N worm and sector was used until 1947. After that a worm and nut type was used.

Engine Air Intake: Early E27Ns used Fordson N type oil bath cleaners. Later, Burgess cylindrical oil bath air cleaners were used.

Grille: Incorporated to modernize the looks, also changed was the radiator top-tank. A Perkins

A rare three-wheel row crop conversion of a 1949 E27N Fordson. The conversion was done by Bettison of Holbeach, Lincolnshire. It is owned by P. Timms of Harefield, Middlesex.

Here is one of only twenty-five Fordson E27N Roadless conversions, this one owned by S.P. Ridges, Trotten, South Hampton. It is also one of thirteen built to operate on TVO; the remaining twelve were diesel.

badge was fitted on diesel models.

Electrical: Prior to 1946, Model N lights and generator could be fitted. After 1946, 12 volt lights and a starter were available.

Serial Numbers

Year	Beginning Serial Number
1945	980520
1946	993489
1947	1018979
1948	1054094
1949	1104657

Year	Beginning Serial Number
1950	1138033
1951	1180610
1952	1216575

Records indicate the last E27N was Serial Number 1216990.

The Fordson Major, Power Major, and Super Major

The biggest impact the Fordson E27N Major had on the tractor world was the normalizing of diesel power. Prior to the E27N, diesels were

S.P. Ridges drives his E27N Roadless conversion at The Great Dorset Steam Fair in 1993. Restoration was begun in 1973 after the tractor was found abandoned in the woods near Newbury.

A line of four E27Ns with Perkins diesels at The Great Dorset Steam Fair in 1993.

This 1953 Fordson New Major is almost hidden by its loader. It was by this model that Ford entered the diesel tractor market. It was also the first Ford tractor in the United States to be painted blue.

thought to be too costly and temperamental for routine farm use.

Even before Frank Perkins had installed his diesel engine in his E27N, the engineers at Dagenham had decided that diesel was the wave of the future. In 1944, Ford Motor Company, Ltd., General Manager Patrick Hennessey had authorized the design of a new tractor utilizing an engine that would be offered in a diesel version as well as in gasoline and TVO (Tractor Vaporizing Oil) versions. Material restrictions and development delays resulted in the E27N being offered as a stop gap when World War II was over. The "New" Major, as they were called, would not be ready until 1952.

The New Major's three engines used the same

The Fordson New Major was available in gasoline, TVO (Tractor Vaporizing Oil), or diesel versions. This 1953 model has the 220ci diesel. It was Ford's first venture into the diesel engine business, and it has a good reputation for dependability and power.

NEW! Fordson Dexta Diesel

ONLY $1⁶⁰ FOR FUEL – PLOW ALL DAY!*

Fuel bills running high? Then try a Fordson Dexta Diesel tractor. Now you can reduce your fuel bills as much as 50 percent—and even more! In addition, you can enjoy the extra lugging ability of a diesel engine. And you can save on upkeep and repair expense, too—the Fordson Dexta Diesel tractor is an "easy keeper."

But here's the best part: The new Fordson Dexta Diesel tractor is in the same price range as comparable *gasoline* tractors of other makes—yet it usually cuts fuel costs in *half*, and more. A typical Ford value!

The Fordson Dexta Diesel comes fully equipped, too—including standard hydraulic system and 3-point hitch for Ford tools, six-speed transmission, power take-off, Proof-Meter, lights, and much more. Live PTO is also available.

So see your nearby Ford tractor and implement dealer and get the facts. Better yet, try out the new Fordson Dexta Diesel on your own farm. *The sooner* *you put it to work, the sooner you can start saving on* *fuel bills!* Convenient terms can be arranged—up to four crop years to pay. Ask your dealer.

Also See World's Largest Selling Diesel Tractor

FORDSON POWER MAJOR

Full 4-plow power. Used by more farmers the world over than any other diesel tractor. See your Ford tractor dealer and find out why. Save plenty!

Tractor and Implement Division • Ford Motor Company • Birmingham, Michigan

FORD

LOW COST FARMING AT ITS BEST!

*Based on 10-hour day; 1½c fuel; average soil.

Plow all day for $1.60. The fine print says the daily fuel cost is based on 16 cents-per-gallon diesel fuel. This is enough to bring tears to the eyes of today's farmer.

Modifications and conversions of every kind appeared at The 1993 Great Dorset Steam Fair. This is a very neat turbocharged Fordson Major.

block and crank. Compression ratios ranged from 4.35:1 for TVO to 16:1 for the diesel (5.5:1 for gasoline). The later versions, the Power Major and Super Major featured horsepower increases. Diesel versions had a displacement advantage over the gasoline and TVO versions. By 1960, over 90 percent of the production was diesel.

The new tractor was much larger and heavier than the E27N. It used a three-speed transmission with a two-range shifter, giving it six forward speeds and two in reverse.

Collecting Comments

Fordson New Majors, Power Majors, and Super Majors have not really caught on as collector tractors, especially the older versions with their rather drab styling and paint. The Ford 5000 Super Major (known in the United Kingdom as the New Performance Super Major) is gaining in popularity, however. This model and the Super Major have live PTO and hydraulics, the differential lock, disk brakes, and a draft-control three-point hitch.

Here is a Fordson Triple D (Doe Dual Drive) that was converted at Maldon, Essex, England, in the days before four-wheel-drive tractors were readily available.

This 1959 ad boasts of cutting fuel costs by 50 percent by going diesel.

Characteristics of the New Major,
Power Major, and Super Major:

Engine: Ford-built, gasoline and TVO: 3.740x4.524in bore and stroke, 199ci, four-cylinder, OHV, rated at 1600rpm. Diesel: 3.938x 4.524in bore and stroke, 220ci four-cylinder, OHV, rated at 1600rpm for the New Major and Power Major, and at 1700rpm for Super Majors. Pressure lubrication system. Water pump cooling.

Weight: 5,100lb (gas), 5,300lb (diesel).

Transmission: 6 speeds forward, 2 reverse

Final Drive: Spiral bevel pinion with individual bull gears

Brakes: Independent brakes on each rear wheel. Disk brakes on the Super Major

Standard equipment: Fenders; Pneumatic tires (front, 7.50x16; rear, 11.00x38); hydraulics; The Hydraulic Power Lift System did not provide draft control on the New Major or Power Major.

Paint: Medium blue with red wheels and trim. Blue and beige for the Ford 5000 Super Major

Steering: Power steering available, all models

Electrical: 12-volt system

Known as the Ploughmaster 6, the Super Major conversion offers mechanical front wheel assist. It was photographed at The Great Dorset Steam Fair in 1993.

England's answer to Palmer Fossum's Funk V-8 8N. This 1964 Fordson Super Major has a 200bhp Perkins 510ci V-8 diesel. It has disc air brakes and four speeds forward plus overdrive. The conversion is by Vincent Engineering, which claims it has a top speed of 60mph (even with a 3-bottom plow?). The Vincent Fordson appeared at the 1993 Great Dorset Steam Fair. The owner and builder is Richard Vincent, Henstridge, Somerset, England.

This is a 1952 County Crawler FC conversion of a Fordson Major diesel. It is owned by David Hastings of Billesdon, Leicestershire, who did the restoration.

Serial Numbers

Year	Beginning Serial Number
New Major Series	
1953	1,247,381
1954	1,276,857
1955	1,322,525
1956	1,371,418
1957	1,412,409
1958	1,458,381
Power Major Series	
1958	1,481,091
1959	1,494,448
1960	1,538,065
1961	1,583,906
Super Major Series	
1961	08A-300001-M
1962	08B-740000-A
1963	08C-781370-A
1964	08D-900000

The 1960 Dexta was an advanced tractor for its time. Besides the three-cylinder diesel engine, it boasted (on the tag on the grille) live hydraulics and live PTO.

A 1967 Ford 2000. In 1965, Ford switched to a 158ci three-cylinder engine for this model. It was rated at 31 PTO horsepower at 1900rpm.

A 1962 Fordson Super Dexta powered by a Perkins-built three-cylinder diesel of 152.7ci engine. At rated speed, 2250rpm, 38.83 PTO horse-power is produced, according to the University of Nebraska tests.

The Ford Diesel 2000 is identical to the Fordson Super Dexta. With the establishment of the Ford Tractor Division of the Ford Motor Company in 1962, Super Dextas were imported and identified as shown here. This one is owned by Dr. Jack Garner of Aledo, Texas.

Dr. Jack Garner of Aledo, Texas, finds his Ford Diesel 2000 (Super Dexta) ideal for keeping his acreage mowed.

The lift system of the Super Dexta is much the same as that of the 8N Ford. The Super Dexta's live hydraulics are directly driven by the engine.

The Super Dexta Ford Diesel 2000 has a two-stage clutch. The first stage disconnects the drive-train; the second stage disconnects the live PTO. This requires a fairly long throw for the clutch pedal. Dr. Jack Garner, a mechanical engineering manager at Lockheed Aircraft, demonstrates how high the clutch pedal is when in the full-up position.

The Super Dexta Ford 2000 has a three-speed transmission with a two-speed auxiliary, giving it six forward speeds. Top gear gives it a speed of over 17mph at 2000rpm. Also shown just in front of the seat is a selector valve and outlet for a remote cylinder. Note how high the clutch pedal is in the fully released position.

The Fordson Dexta and Super Dexta

In 1957, British Ford finally built their Ford-Ferguson. It wasn't a real Ford-Ferguson, of course, but the new Fordson Dexta. It marked Ford, UK's reentry into the compact tractor market. The new Dexta had a silhouette much like that of the N Series American Fords. It was rated at 32hp and had three-point hitch.

The Dexta's three-cylinder Perkins diesel engine was rated at 2000rpm. It was coupled to a three-speed with two-range gearbox giving six speeds forward and two in reverse. Live PTO and hydraulics were options. In most soils, the Dexta could handle a three-bottom plow. The hydraulic controls were designed to accommodate remote double-acting cylinders as well as the three-point hitch. The hitch had a lift capacity of 1,850lb at the uni-balls.

As with the American N Series tractors, the Dexta used radius rods and adjustable-length front axles. The rear wheels were power adjustable. Bull gears were not used on the rear axles, again like the N Series.

The Super Dexta, introduced in 1962, had a displacement increase and an increase in rated rpm. The Super Dexta was imported as the Ford 2000 Diesel between 1962 and 1964.

Collecting Comments

The Dexta, Super Dexta, and Ford 2000 Diesel have become quintessential additions to the major Ford tractor collections. They are also much desired by the landscaper, truck gardener, and estate owner because of their modern features and diesel engines. They are also desirable because, as yet, their prices are below that of comparable Ford 601 and 801 tractors.

Characteristics of the Fordson Dexta and Super Dexta:
Engine: Dexta, Perkins-built, 3.5x5.0in bore and stroke, 144ci, three-cylinder, OHV, rated at 2000rpm. Super Dexta, Perkins-built, 3.6x5.0in bore

Features of the Super Dexta's controls. Note the dual brake pedals that can be locked together. Just behind the brakes is a differential lock pedal.

Inboard of the hydraulic control quadrant is the toggle for shifting between draft control and position control.

Above and Right
On his 1962 Ford Diesel 2000, Dr. Jack Garner has devised a parallel linkage for the three-point hitch which keeps the hitch ball "level" as the hitch is raised. This allows him to pick up heavy-tongue trailers for maneuvering them around his yard without dismounting to latch the ball.

The left side view of Dr. Jack Garner's Fordson Super Dexta/Ford Diesel 2000. The Super Dexta weighs in at a little over 3,000lb without ballast.

and stroke, 152.7ci, three-cylinder, OHV, rated at 2000rpm. Pressure lubrication system. Water pump cooling.

    Weight: 3,000lb

    Transmission: 6 speeds forward, 2 reverse

    Final Drive: Spiral bevel pinion. Differential lock on the Super Dexta

    Brakes: Independent drum brakes on each rear wheel

    Standard equipment: Fenders; pneumatic tires (front, 5.50x16; rear, 12.4x28); hydraulics, live; position and draft control.

    Paint: Medium blue with red wheels and trim. Blue and beige for the Ford 2000 Diesel (Super Dexta)

    Steering: Worm and Nut

    Electrical: 12-volt system

    PTO: Live, 2-stage clutch

Author Robert N. Pripps (left) and Dr. Jack Garner (seated on tractor) pose with Garner's Ford Diesel 2000/Super Dexta. Garner uses the tractor with either a post hole digger or a Bush-Hog mower on his Aledo, Texas, ranch.

The Fordson three-cylinder Dexta diesel is one of the slickest tractors made by Ford, with six forward speeds, live hydraulics and PTO, and even a 12 volt electrical system. Shown is a 1960 model.

The Dexta, announced in late 1957, was about midway between the 600 and 800 series US-built Fords. But the Dexta was a diesel. Ford soon offered domestic diesels as well, but the three-cylin-der Dexta model set the pace for the future. The badge on the grille declares that this tractor has live hydraulics and live PTO.

In appearance the Dexta is essentially the same as the Super Dexta except on the Super Dexta the headlights are in the grille (making it easier to mount a loader). The Dexta used a 144ci three-cylinder engine, while the one in the Super Dexta displaced 153ci.

The Dexta was tested at the University of Nebraska in 1959, Test Number 684. The Super Dexta was not tested by the University of Nebraska. The name "Dexta" comes from the Greek word *dexios*, which has to do with being on the right, or right handed. The name implies adroitness, capability, and competence. The word "dexterity" comes from the same root.

The Dexta (and Super Dexta) tractors have a
tachometer with a recording hour-meter.

Serial Numbers

Year	Beginning Serial Number	Year	Beginning Serial Number
Fordson Dexta		*Fordson Super Dexta*	
1958	16066	1961	09A 312001M
1959	20427	1962	09B 070000A
1960	46212	1963	09C 731454A
1961	72003	1964	09D 9000000A

Chapter 6

Ford Tractors, Red and Gray— Models 8N, NAA, and Series 500 through 800

Model 8N 1947-1952	
★★★★★	Serial No. 1-250
★★★★	Serial No. 251-1000
★★★	Serial No. 1001-9999
★★	Serial No. 10000-263843
★★★	Serial No. 263844-442034
★★★★	Serial No. 442035-524000
★★★★★	Serial No. 524001 and up

For 8NAN Models, add a star, unless already a five-star

Model NAA Jubilee	
★★★★	Serial No. 1-999
★★★	Serial No. 1000-128000
★★★★	Serial No. 128000 and up

(Records indicate that 51,490 Jubilees were made in 1954, meaning the last serial number would be NAA128965.)

Basic Model Number					
	5—	6—	7—	8—	9—
Middle Number					
-1-	★★★	★★	★★★	★★	★★
-2-	★★	★	★★	★	★
-3-	★★	★	★★	★	★
-4-	★★★★	★★	★★★	★★	★★
-5-	★★★★	★★	★★★	★★	★★
-6-	★★★★	★★★	★★★★	★★★	★★★
-7-	★★★★	★★★	★★★★	★★★	★★★
-8-	★★★★	★★★	★★★★	★★★★	★★★★

Last number —0 = built between 1955 and 1958
Last number —1 = built between 1958 and 1961

The turbulence within the Ford Motor Company following the death of Edsel in 1943 was not generally seen outside the company. The aging founder, Henry Ford, resumed the position of president that had been held by his son. Henry Ford II was appointed executive vice president on April 28, 1944. Harry H. Bennett was vice president and director of industrial relations.

In fact, the elder Mr. Ford was in poor health and remained most of the time at his Fair Lane Estate. Despite the fact that he was executive VP, Young Henry had to wrest control of day-to-day operations away from Mr. Bennett, who was the only one who routinely had access to the senior Mr. Ford. In some cases, it was suspected, Bennett didn't contact Ford, but just declared, "This is what Henry wants." Finally Young Henry, with the backing of much of the board, used his position as grandson to see Henry Ford. He was able to convince Old Henry that family lineage was on the line and that to protect family interests, he, Henry Ford II, had to be named president.

Thus, on September 21, 1945, the elder Henry Ford resigned the presidency of the Ford Motor Company for the second time and Henry Ford II was named to succeed him. On October 1, 1945, Harry Bennett was replaced by John Bugas, a former FBI agent in Detroit.

World War II was over on September 2, 1945, when Japan formally surrendered. All of Ford Motor Company's business had been disrupted during the war by military production. June saw the last of the giant B-24s roll off the line at the Wil-low Run plant. In two years and ten months 8,685 of the four-engined planes had been built—a testimony to the production genius of Charles Sorensen. In 1945, Ford had no plans for use of the $100 million facility.

Tractor operations were probably the least affected by the war effort, as tractor production was considered more and more essential. In 1945, production of the Model 2N hit 28,729 units. While this was not much for Ford, it was a lot for the tractor industry, and was Ford's second biggest war year.

When Henry Ford II took over, he had to take drastic action to stem the financial hemorrhage.

A nice 1949 Ford 8N with an Arps rock rake is photographed in Door County, Wisconsin. The tractor had Sunday off from its nearby construction project.

A 1952 Ford 8N with a Ford Model 907 flail mower.

The tractor operation came in for scrutiny, as it was seen as never having been profitable. The arrangement with Harry Ferguson was untenable, since it left Ford with no control over the marketing of its product. Options were considered, such as a buyout in whole, or part, of Ferguson. Harry Ferguson was not amenable to any of these overtures, since he had things just the way he wanted them.

On September 5, 1946, the Ford Motor Company announced that after the next June 30, it would discontinue the manufacture of the tractor for Harry Ferguson, Inc., and would build an improved tractor for distribution through independent dealers.

Henry Ford, 1863-1947

Henry Ford, automobile manufacturing genius, died April 7, 1947, at the age of 83. According to newspaper accounts, he went to bed as usual at 9 p.m., after inspecting the flood waters from a spring storm inundating a corner of his Fair Lane Estate. At 11:15 he awoke feeling ill and thirsty. Clara, his wife of fifty-nine years, brought him a drink of water. Then, some time after midnight, the man who put the world on wheels died quietly in a chilly room lit only by kerosene lamps (the storm had knocked out power to Fair Lane). Henry Ford left this world as he came in—a scene not that different from his Michigan farmhouse birth.

A fine example of a 1952 8N. This one belongs to Dwight Emstrom of Galesburg, Illinois. Note the tabs at the top corners of the grille; these are for tipping the grille forward to clean chaff from the radiator.

Dwight Emstrom and his 1952 8N at his Galesburg, Illinois, spread. Emstrom is a collector and restorer of classic tractors, especially Fords. He also sells parts and implements for Fords and Ford-Fergusons.

A Dearborn cord wood saw mounted on an 8N, ready to use.

A 1952 8N with its Dearborn cord wood saw in the raised position. This outfit belongs to Dwight Emstrom of Galesburg, Illinois.

Ford was buried on a family plot located a short distance from where he was born. Today, the plot is on the front lawn of St. Martha's Episcopal Church, which was built a decade after his death. Ford's fortune was estimated at $500 million. After settlement of the will, Clara Ford held 55 percent of the voting stock and Edsel's widow, Eleanor, held 52.4 percent.

As an example of the esteem in which Henry Ford was held by the general public, the following vignette by Edgar A. Guest is included:

"We are all his debtors now. There is none of us, rich or poor, in humble or high place, whose life has not been bettered by his labor. He came into the world when the backs of men were weary and heavy-laden. By the dreams he had, pursued and achieved, the burdens of drudgery were taken from the shoulders of the humble and given to steel and wheel."

The Birth of the Model 8N

On November 26, 1946, about two weeks after Harry Ferguson was notified that the Handshake Agreement was to be discontinued, Henry Ford II announced the formation of Dearborn Motors to market a new tractor model. The 8N was to be ready for the 1948 model year. Dearborn was to design and build a completely new line of implements, as well.

The following January (1947), Harry Ferguson leveled a lawsuit against the Ford Motor Company for $251 million. There were actually two suits: First, Ford was charged with seeking to create a small-tractor monopoly, resulting in making Ferguson's business unprofitable; and, second, Ford was charged with infringement of Ferguson's patents. Henry Ford II said, "The blunt truth is the Ford-Ferguson deal made Harry Ferguson a multi-millionaire and cost Ford $25 million."

A nicely painted 1952 Ford 8N on the sales lot at Polacek Implement in Phillips, Wisconsin. Completely refurbished, it was for sale for $2,400.

This working 8N is owned by Bill Dean of Waverly, Iowa. The name of his place is—you guessed it—Candy Stripe Acres. The tractor, serial number 500682, is a 1952 model.

An 8N Ford stripped of its sheet metal for restoration. The unusual front wheels are to support the additional weight of a loader.

Most 8N flywheel housings carry this casting designation.

Radius rods are attached to the front, or movable, portion of the front axle on 9Ns and 2Ns and on Ford tractors of the late sixties. On 8Ns and up through the early sixties, they were attached to the rear fixed portion of the front axle. This was a concession to the Ferguson patents. The Ferguson type provides greater strength at wide settings.

Shena, the German shepherd, watches approvingly as Palmer Fossum guides the Funk V-8 8N into the furrow. The Ford-Funk will haul plow like no other tractor of the forties.

The engine of Palmer Fossum's 1949 Ford-Funk V-8 is the 95hp Mercury (or Ford truck) 8BA model. The dual straight-pipes set up a cacophonous cackle.

Palmer Fossum and his 1949 Ford-Funk V-8 are silhouetted against the Minnesota sky and prairie. These conversions of the Ford tractor were made by the Industrial Division of the Funk Aircraft Company of Coffeeville, Kansas.

Pulling three "sixteens" at a fast walk through hard virgin stubble is a feat not accomplished by many tractors of the forties. But then, most tractors of that period were not equipped with a 100hp, 239ci, V-8 engine. Palmer Fossum is shown on his 1949 Ford-Funk conversion, breaking the middle furrows of the field being plowed. Needless to say, the two straight-pipes were snorting.

Both the left and right brakes are on the right side of the 8N tractor, a great improvement over the 9N and 2N. The pedals can be operated simultaneously or individually.

Palmer Fossum, shown in the cab, uses this 8N Funk six-cylinder conversion for garden and lawn work around his Northfield, Minnesota, farm home. The tractor has a special high-low speed auxiliary transmission to handle tilling and highway speeds. It is also equipped with a special chain-drive PTO to keep the tiller at proper rotational speed while the tractor creeps.

Fossum's 8N Funk conversion uses the 226ci Ford L-head industrial engine. The engine is rated at 95hp at 3600rpm, which is plenty for the rototiller application. The engine is governed at a more reasonable 2200rpm, however, to extend the life of both the tractor and the tiller.

While introduction of the new 8N was still six months away, the suit anticipated the patent conflicts. The facts were that many of the design ideas had been jointly thought up, or had been thought up by Ford people, but Ferguson went ahead with patents. The front wheel adjustment idea was not used on the 8N, although what was used looks similar. Patents for the three-point linkage and draft control were running out, anyway. The real bone of contention was the hydraulic control system that controlled flow by restricting the supply-side of the pump. Ford engineers had always considered that to be the hard way to do the job, but didn't have time to change it for the 8N.

Hydraulic control was the only point on which Ferguson won. In an out-of-court settlement approved by the court, Ford was instructed to stop using supply-side control by the end of the 1952 model year. The success of Ferguson's tractor business belied loss of business damages. The settlement was for $9.25 million, a fraction of the amount Ford had spent in its defense.

Nevertheless, in the early days of 1947, the successful outcome of the suit was not a foregone conclusion. Designers went ahead, as did those involved in Dearborn Motors, not knowing for sure if they would have a tractor to sell. In July of that year, the tractor and implements were ready. Model 2N production stopped and 8N production took over. The enthusiastic reception of farmers made 1947 the best for tractor production in twenty years.

Collecting Comments

Although newer than the Ford-Ferguson, the 8N is just as much desired by the collectors. The

Left and Below
The differences between early and late 8N instrument panels are shown in these two pictures. Starting in mid-1950 (at serial number 290271), the ProofMeter was added below the choke button. Also note the removable shift knob on the later series.

reason seems to be that the 8N contains so many important improvements. A second reason could be that the red and light gray paint produces a much more appealing appearance. Early and late serial numbers are more in demand, of course. Accessories such as the Ford-accessory over/under-drive and headlights add value, as does an appropriate Dearborn implement.

In July 1947, Dearborn Motors introduced the new Ford tractor, the 8N. A complete line of new implements was also available. The Ford-Ferguson model was phased out at that time. The new tractor was a classic engineering masterpiece for which the demand has not slackened in over forty-five years. It was basically the same size and shape as the Ford-Ferguson and had the same styling, but it now had bright red cast iron and a lighter gray (to hide bird droppings) sheet metal. Two other major

differences were a four, rather than three, speed transmission; and brake pedals that were now both on the right side and could be actuated together.

Funk Conversions

Midway through production of the 8N, the Funk Aircraft Company of Coffeeville, Kansas, began marketing conversions for Ford tractors wherein the four-cylinder engine was replaced by either the 226ci 90-95hp six, or by the 239ci 95-100hp V-8. According to Funk advertising of the day, these tractors could be used to pull three-bottom plows and other heavy implements, so they must have felt the transmission and differential were strong enough to handle the extra power. Naturally, the engines were governed at speeds

With the 8N came the toggle-lever control (shown under the seat) for shifting between draft control and position control. In the draft control mode, increasing draft loads on the implement tended to hydraulically raise the implement until the original set load was restored. In the position mode, draft control was blocked out and the implement remained in the same position with respect to the tractor regardless of load. 9Ns and 2Ns did not have this feature.

approximating that of the four-cylinder, so only about half the advertised engine power was actually available. Most Funk-Fords were used for heavy power take-off jobs, such as mowing, pumping, and driving a thresher, where at least some of the power did not go through the gears.

The conversion of Ford tractors (Ford-Fergusons can also be converted) with the Funk kits is complex. Since the tractor has no frame, an axle mount was included on the front of the four-cylinder engine. The axle mount had to be added to the larger engines. The larger radiators and higher engines required the hoods to be higher. The engines being longer required the radius rods and steering rods to be extended, and a hood extension was supplied to reach the dash.

The Funk-Fords are interesting to the collector and, if in good shape, would rate an extra star, that is, for the six-cylinder version. The eight-cylinder version is quite rare; also, its exhaust note is so intriguing that any Funk V-8 is automatically a five-star.

Characteristics of the 1947 Model 8N:

Engine: Ford-built, 3.187x3.75in bore and stroke, 119.7ci, four-cylinder, L-head, rated at 2000rpm. Novi flyball governor capable of governing to 2200rpm. Pressurized lubrication system with full-flow cartridge-type filter. Water pump cooling. Compression ratio, 6:1 early, 6.7:1 late (gasoline), 4.75:1 for 8NAN which resulted in less power

Weight: 2,410lb early, 2,490lb late

Transmission: four speeds forward, one reverse

Final Drive: Spiral bevel gear drive with straddle-mounted pinion, 6.66:1 ratio

Brakes: Independent brakes on each rear wheel controlled by pedals on the right side of the tractor; no means to lock pedals together, although both pedals could be depressed together by the right foot. No clutch pedal interconnect to brake.

Standard equipment: Fenders; pneumatic tires front, 4.00x19, 6.00x16 optional late; rear, 10x28

Hydraulic Implement Control: A four-cylinder scotch yoke pump supplied pressure to a rockshaft ram. The pressure flow is controlled by a servo valve. The position of the valve handle corresponds to the position of the implement. There is therefore no "neutral" position, as is the case with other systems. The valve is also controlled by the draft linkage which effects the patented Draft Control. The valve functions to cut off flow to the supply side of the pump, rather than the pressure side, as is common. Besides draft control, a toggle lever under the seat can select "Position Control." With this lever

The three-hole upper link draft control attach point mechanism characteristic of late 8Ns.

actuated, draft control is blocked out and implement position is controlled strictly by the quadrant.

Paint: Light gray sheet metal and bright red cast iron

Steering: Recirculating ball replacing the sector gears of the Ford-Ferguson. A higher steering wheel, a flip-up seat, and running boards allowed for operation while standing.

Wheels: Rears consist of rounded center disc rather than the flat type used on the Ford-Ferguson; same type rim. Front and rear wheels now bolted at hub, rather than being bolted to a plate hub as on the Ford-Ferguson.

Engine Air Intake: A screened grill air intake was positioned on the right aft hood

Hood Script and Emblem: Ford script trademark embossed on the front of both sides of the hood; the Ford oval emblem in the front center of the hood was now larger than that of the Ford-Ferguson and was chrome with a red background

Grille: Tip-out type, for radiator cleaning

A more conventional side-mount distributor was added to 8Ns in 1951. This change made replacing and setting the points much easier.

Late model 8Ns have an improved rear wheel seal as indicated by the slight bulge below the axle. Leaking rear wheel seals had been the nemesis of the brakes on 9N, 2N, and 8N tractors before this improvement.

The fuel tank from an extremely rare 1952 Ford 8NAN. The two filler caps are labeled "GAS" and "KER" (for kerosene). The tractor, owned by Palmer Fossum, is undergoing complete restoration.

The characteristic hex-head nut found on the ends of 8N and Jubilee rear axles.

The underside of the 8NAN two-compartment fuel tank. The special valve is for switching from gasoline to kerosene after starting.

Interview with Harold Brock

Harold Brock is generally credited as the "designer" of the Ford N-series tractors. Of course, like all big-company operations, many people contribute to a design, but Brock was the design team leader, and his actual title was program manager. As such, he worked for Chief Engineer Lawrence Sheldrick.

Harold Brock started at Ford when he enrolled in 1929 in the Henry Ford Trade School, a technical high school. In this program, he worked in the shop for three weeks and went to class one week per month, learning all trades as well as getting a high school diploma. Upon receipt of the diploma, Brock elected to stay in the program, taking up the engineering curriculum. Toward the end of that time, he worked closely with Henry Ford. Finally, in 1938, at age 26, he was given responsibility for the tractor program. Here are Harold Brock's recollections of those days:

"To get the program going, a group of forty-five of us were moved from Dearborn to the Rouge plant so we'd be more isolated. A small group stayed at Dearborn to interface with the rest of the company. The basic tractor layout represented previous experience with the Fordson in that the unified [frame-less] design was to be used. The Ferguson-Brown and the Ferguson black tractor were not of much use as they were too small and light to be much more than models.

"Chief Engineer Sheldrick, Henry Ford, Charles Sorensen, and Harry Ferguson were in daily consultation, as was Ferguson's man John Chambers. Ferguson had another engineer, Willie Sands, but he spent most of his time in Ireland. There were no formal meetings; people would come by and make suggestions. I had to sort them out and use the best. Mr. Ford would come in every morning with ideas he had thought of during the evening. Then he'd come back in the afternoon to see how they'd been incorporated. Ford, too, liked to come to Rouge to get away. Thomas Edison used to come in once in awhile, too. Neither Mr. Ford, nor Harry Ferguson, were very good at reading the drawings we were making. For explaining them, we often had to color the drawings with colored pencils so they could see the various parts.

"The layout of the tractor had several factors considered. It had to be heavy enough and low enough for stability, especially with the implement up for transport. We estimated the weight of the heaviest implement and sized the hydraulics accordingly. The implements were tucked in as tight behind the tractor as possible.

"Cost and mass production were constant drivers. As many car and truck parts as possible were used. Options were kept to a minimum, so that extra parts would not have to be stocked. Mr. Ford instructed me to make the length of the tractor such that it would fit crosswise in a boxcar, which I did. We could get fourteen in a boxcar. Other tractor companies had to use flat cars, and because of their various models, never could utilize the available space as well.

"We had in mind a real utility tractor, and made crop clearance as much as possible while keeping the profile low so that it could be used in orchards. We wanted to keep the operator low for his protection and so he could get under the trees. Our competition was not other tractor brands. We felt our competition, at least back in 1938, was the horse.

"Power required was determined by that required to pull two 14in plows in average soil in second gear. This provided reasonable tillage speed. More power would have wasted gas; less would have operated the plow too slowly. By making the tractor light, less power was consumed just to carry the tractor over the ground. Some brands of tractors required 25 percent of their power just to move the tractor. An L-head engine was chosen because it was much cheaper and required less maintenance before hydraulic lifters were invented.

"Work on the 8N began in 1945. We didn't see much of Henry Ford after 1943. Henry Ford II was instrumental in hiring the new management which broke off the relationship with Ferguson.

"The hydraulic system was based upon the Ferguson-Brown design, although that design had problems. The drawings were all made by Ford; Ferguson later took out patents. We didn't like the suction-side pump control, as it starved the pump. The only reason it worked was because there was enough leakage in the valve to keep the pump lubricated. Originally, the system operated on 1,500psi pressure; later that went to 2,000psi."

It is interesting to know that Brock was also instrumental in designing the World War II Jeep. He claims his group was calling it the Jeep, because of its designation "GP," before anyone else. Also during World War II, he worked on dual overhead cam V-8 and V-12 engines, for which Sorensen was casting one-piece blocks.

After the new management was in place in the fifties, the size of the staff increased dramatically. People were hired from other tractor companies, and, according to Brock, models and options proliferated, costs went up, and volume down. Brock left Ford and went to John Deere in 1959.

It is also interesting to know that Brock's wife, Kathleen, whom he married after his first wife died, had also been a Ford employee and had been a clerk for Henry Ford. She had worked in the same area as Harold during the war. Some time after Brock's first wife had died, he was to speak at an SAE function in Detroit. One of his former Ford associates asked him if he knew Kathleen was in the area. Harold had not seen her since the old days, but looked her up, and the rest is history.

The special vaporizer manifold on the rare 8NAN. The head is also different; it's of lower compression ratio than the standard 8N head. This photo is of Palmer Fossum's 1952 model. Note the side distributor and the ProofMeter cable, significant of late-model 8Ns.

Year by Year Changes

Changes introduced for 1948
- A different clutch linkage is used
- The top-link rocker, which actuates the draft control, now has three moment arm positions, rather than one.

Changes for 1949
- Adjustable recirculating ball mechanism after S/N 216998

Changes for 1950
- 6.00x16 front tires an option

110

Palmer Fossum, Northfield, Minnesota, grades his driveway with a Ford Model 600 on Arps tracks. Fossum also uses the front blade for light dozing and snow plowing. He claims the traction is about as good as four-wheel drive and that flotation is excellent on soft ground.

- Chrome front hood emblem replaced by argent
- Side distributor/coil after S/N 263844
- Removable shift knob replaces knob cast with lever
- Over/underdrive auxiliary transmission appears as an option
- ProofMeter tachometer appears at S/N 290271

Changes for 1951
- Ford script trademark is embossed on fenders as well as hood

Changes for 1952
- Improved rear axle seal introduced midyear
- Rear axle has a bulge at lower outer extremity
- High-Direct-Low auxiliary transmission became a Ford-supplied option

Serial Numbers

Year	Serial Numbers
8N	
1947	1 to 37907
1948	37908 to 141369
1949	141370 to 245636
1950	245637 to 343592
1951	343593 to 442034
1952	442035 to 524076

All 8Ns that have the ProofMeter have this panel opposite for a temperature gauge, but only 8NAN kerosene burners had the gauge as standard equipment. The placard reads, "Do not use distillate fuel except when the hand is on green."

The Model NAA

When the Ford-Ferguson lawsuit was settled in 1952, Ford engineers had already been planning an improved tractor for introduction in 1953—Ford Motor Company's fiftieth anniversary. Prominent on the hood of the restyled tractor was a circular emblem that said "Golden Jubilee Model 1903-1953." Thus, the Model NAA soon came to be known as the Jubilee. Golden referred to the fiftieth anniversary of the company; Jubilee is a biblical term having to do with fifty year periods (see Leviticus 25:11).

Production of the new Jubilee began in January 1953. This model was larger and heavier and sported a totally new overhead valve four-cylinder engine. Also, it was completely restyled so that it no longer resembled previous Ford tractors, or the Ferguson TO-30, which came out in 1951 and was stiff competition for the 8N.

An interesting new "live," or direct engine-driven, hydraulic pump and system was incorporated, eliminating conflict with the Ferguson patents. Originally, a vane pump was used, mounted under the hood alongside the engine. A flow-control valve, called the Hy-trol, was included to make the system more, or less, sensitive. Later, a piston-type pump was substituted. A separate hydraulic reservoir was provided, as were provisions for remote hydraulic cylinders.

A non-live PTO was retained as standard on the Jubilee, but a live PTO was offered as an option. The live PTO was operated by a hydraulic clutch; the clutch was operated by a separate pump; the pump was operated by the cable that drove the ProofMeter. Needless to say, this was not a common option.

The new 134ci engine was advertised as the "Red Tiger." It produced a maximum belt horsepower of 30.15 at 2000rpm during the University of Nebraska tests.

The Jubilee also had improved brakes and rear axle seals over the 8N, and an improved governor.

One of the most desirable combinations: a Jubilee with a good full-control loader. This one is a 1953 model owned by Kevin Kelly of Rochester, Minnesota.

1953 Jubilees can be distinguished from look-alike Model 600s by the nose medallion. It says "Golden Jubilee Model 1903-1953," Ford Motor Company's fiftieth anniversary. Jubilee is a biblical term having to do with fifty-year periods (see Leviticus 25:11). Interestingly, the Bible states that there was to be no cultivation of the land during the Jewish year of Jubilee.

The muffler was relocated to a spot under the hood, alongside the engine. This reduced the possibility of the muffler causing fires in dry straw, and also allowed for optional vertical exhausts. The instrument panel now contained a temperature gage as standard equipment.

On May 30, 1953, with the Ferguson lawsuit settled, Ford Motor Company acquired the assets of Dearborn Motors. The Tractor and Implement Division was then organized.

The 1954 version can be distinguished from the 1953 model by its revised star-encircled nose medallion. Internally, the 1954 version had gear ratio changes which produced a reduction in operating speed for a given engine rpm.

Jubilee tractors were painted the same as the 8Ns.

Collecting Comments

For some reason, collectors hold Ford NAA tractors in very high regard. This is probably because they represent the culmination of the basic N-Series design. Also a factor is that there were only two years of production. For whatever reason, Jubilees are much in demand. There were some NAB distillate-burning models, which are rare enough to rate five stars automatically. There were also Funk conversions to the then-new Ford truck, or industrial, six-cylinder OHV engine. These, too, rate an automatic five stars. Early and late serial numbers are more in demand, of course. Accessories such as the Ford-accessory over/underdrive and headlights add value, as does an appropriate implement.

Characteristics of the Model NAA:
Engine: Ford-built, 3.44x3.60in bore and stroke, 134ci, four-cylinder, OHV, rated at 2000rpm. Flyball governor. Pressurized lubrication system with full-flow cartridge-type filter. Water pump cooling. Compression ratio, 6:6 (gasoline), 4.75:1 for NAB.

Weight: 2,510lb

Transmission: Four speeds forward, one reverse

Final Drive: Spiral bevel gear drive with straddle-mounted pinion.

Brakes: Independent brakes on each rear wheel controlled by pedals on the right side of the tractor

Standard equipment: Fenders; Pneumatic tires (front, 6.00x16, 5.50x16 optional; rear, 10x28)

Hydraulic Implement Control: A vane or piston pump supplies pressure to rock-shaft ram. The pressure flow is controlled by a servo valve. The position of the valve handle corresponds to the position of the implement. There is therefore no "neutral" position, as is the case with other systems. The valve is also controlled by the draft linkage which effects the patented Draft Control. The valve functions to cut off flow to the outlet side of the pump and recirculation-relief valve is used. Besides draft control, a toggle lever under the seat can select "Position Control." With this lever actuated, draft control is blocked out and implement position is controlled strictly by the quadrant. A Hy-trol knob adjusts pump output.

Paint: Light gray sheet metal and bright red cast iron

Steering: Recirculating ball

Wheels: Rears have rounded center disc like the 8N

Engine Air Intake: A screened grille air intake on the left aft hood.

Hood Script and emblem: Ford script trademark embossed in red on the front of both sides of the hood and on the fenders; Emblem is round and in the front center of the hood

Grille: Recessed, tip-out type

Serial Numbers

Year	Beginning Serial Number
1953	NAA 1
1954	NAA 77475

Jubilee (NAA) fenders do not have creases as do 9Ns, 2Ns, and 8Ns. They do have a nut on the ends of the rear axles like the 8N, and unlike the subsequent 600. A well-built back blade, such as the one shown here, is an essential tool for any three-point tractor.

This Model 651 is equipped with Arps tracks. An unbeatable combination for use in snow or mud. Operators report traction is as good or better than that of a four-wheel drive.

A 1959 Ford Model 871 in fairly straight condition.
The "egg-crate" grille was introduced in 1958.

A fine example of a Ford NAA Golden Jubilee Model nearing completion of its restoration. Unfortunately, paint from the unusual front wheels was allowed to run onto the tire.

This 1963 Ford NAA Jubilee has the optional
Selec-Trol valve, ahead of the seat, for operating
remote cylinders. This tractor is owned by Mike
Farrell of Eagle River, Wisconsin.

Palmer Fossum poses his 1954 Model NAA prior to entering the furrow for plowing. The NAA is pulling a two-bottom plow with 16in bottoms.

Operating a Ford tractor with the left hand steering and the right operating the hydraulic control is quite natural. Other brands of tractors had the hydraulic control on the left side, on the panel, or even on the column, but these were eventually changed to be like the original Ford-Ferguson. Actually, Ferguson's prototype tractors pioneered this ergonomically correct arrangement long before ergonomics became a science. Shown here is Palmer Fossum plowing with his 1964 Model NAA.

The 1953 and 1954 Ford Model NAA tractors are the same except for the hood medallion. The 1953 version has "Golden Jubilee Model 1903-1953," while the 1954 version, as shown here, has a series of four-pointed stars. Both years are regularly referred to as Jubilees.

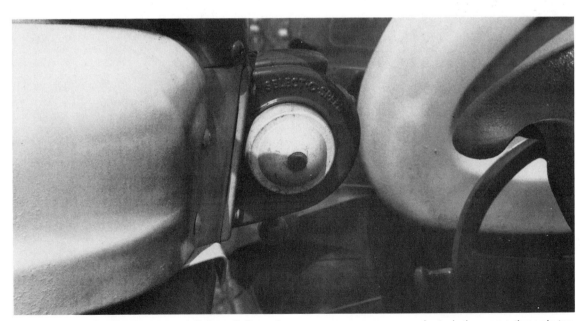

The controller for the ten-speed Select-O-Speed planetary transmission is mounted on center, right under the steering wheel. The control knob is at the bottom in the "Park" position. When this knob is moved up to the horizontal position, first the two reverse gears are selected, then one through ten forward gears. A small foot clutch is used for stopping and starting, but once underway shifting is done by merely moving the knob.

119

After the Jubilee

By 1955, the full impact of the new brand of management at Ford was being felt. It was now ten years since Henry Ford had turned over the reins to his grandson. The Whiz Kids that young Henry had brought in were changing everything.

The success and profit of the Model NAA Jubilee had whetted the appetites of the people in the Tractor and Implement Division, which, more and more, was staffed by personnel hired away from competing tractor companies. "Why be a single-tractor company?" these new managers asked. "Why not expand and compete across the board?" Little by little, the "Any-color-as-long-as-it's-black" policies of Old Henry Ford were dispensed with.

Accordingly, 1955 saw the inclusion of two tractors in the lineup: the Model 600 (134ci) and the Model 800 (172ci). There were three variations of the 600 designated the 640, 650, and 660. The more powerful Model 800, which was Ford's first US-built three-plow tractor, was available as the 850

and 860. All versions were of the utility-tractor configuration, all were equipped with live hydraulics and a three-point hitch. The model designations signified transmission and PTO configurations. The 640, 650, and 850 had transmission (non-live) PTOs, the 660 and 860 had live PTOs. The Model 640 had the four-speed transmission of the Jubilee; the others had a new five-speed transmission. The tractors were the same size and shape as the Jubilee, but the 800s had larger tires and greater engine displacement.

In 1956, models proliferated with the 620 and 820 versions without PTO or three-point lift, and 630 version with lift but no PTO. These three "Special Utility" versions used the four-speed transmission. Also added were the 740, 950, and 960 "Tricycle" versions. The 700 and 900 series were the same as the 600 and 800 except they were of the tricycle configuration. This lineup was then continued through 1957. All of the above were powered by "Red Tiger" overhead valve gasoline engines.

This 1958 Ford Powermaster used a four-cylinder 172ci gasoline engine. LPG and diesel versions were also available. The unit shown has the optional five-speed transmission and live PTO.

800 SERIES
FULL 3-PLOW POWER
—watch the work fly!

5 NEW MODELS

NEW! MOST POWERFUL FORD TRACTOR EVER!

30% More Power to get more work done in less time. Ford's advanced "Red Tiger" engine powers the new 800 Series Ford Tractors—delivers full 3-plow power.

New 5-Speed Transmission* gives a wide range of operating speeds—from less than 2 to over 15 m.p.h. Delivers the power and field speed needed to do better work.

New Live Power Take-off* By pushing regular clutch pedal halfway down, the tractor stops and all the engine power goes to the p.t.o.—reduces stalls and gear shifting.

New Rest-O-Ride Seat* soaks up vibrations, giving you a more comfortable ride. You "float" on a cushion of rubber—smooth riding and restful. Adjustable!

You get advanced FORD features like these...

- Quick attaching of low cost, rear mounted implements
- Choice of hydraulic actions— Constant Draft or Implement Position Control. Two speed settings
- Top link adjustable from tractor seat
- New "Tailored Traction" with easy-on, easy-off wheel weights, sold separately
- Oversize brakes—easier turns; safer, longer wearing
- Headlights and tail light are standard equipment
- Proof-Meter shows hours of operation and travel speed—also r.p.m. of engine, p.t.o. and belt pulley
- Follow-through safety starter

...*and many more outstanding advantages*

*Standard equipment on all new Ford Tractors except Model 640
**Standard equipment on models 600 and 900
***Standard equipment on 800 Series; available at extra cost on 600 Series.

Ford Farming
GETS MORE DONE...AT LOWER COST

1955 ads announce the new 600 and 800 series
tractors.

NEW! Ford Diesel Tractors

NOW! Lowest priced diesel tractors in their class

Many farmers have said, "Sure, we would like to have a diesel tractor and cut our fuel bills in half. But," they add, a diesel tractor costs so much—$550 to $850 more than the same tractor with a gasoline engine. That's a lot of extra money to us."

So Ford set out to solve the problem—to develop a *lower cost* diesel tractor that was practical for the average farmer —one that would fit his pocketbook and do his work for less money per acre—or per hour.

The answer is Ford's new 801 and 901 series diesel tractors —actually the lowest priced diesel tractors in their class. But that's not all. New Ford diesel tractors have all the work saving features for which Ford tractors have long been famous—including Ford's time-tested hydraulic system, power steering and live power take-off as standard equipment on many models.

So see your nearby Ford tractor and implement dealer. Find out how much more you get, how much more you save with a new Ford diesel tractor. Then figure the added profit you'll have at the end of the year with this practical, cost saving power. You'll find it's priced low to help you profit more on *more* farm jobs! Easy terms, too. See them now.

Now! Many Ford tractor models with gasoline, LP-gas and diesel engines

FORD ...low cost farming at its best!

The 1958 grille and paint scheme are shown in this ad announcing the diesel versions of the 801 and 901 models.

Before the end of the 1957 model year, the tractors of the Ford line were given a face-lift and some improved features. To signify the improvements, a 1 was added to each model designator, making, for example, the 640 into the 641. If the 134ci engine was used, the tractor was in the "Workmaster" series; if the 172ci engine was used, it was in the "Powermaster" series.

Liquefied petroleum gas (LPG) variations of each engine were offered. Powermaster and Workmaster diesels became available in 1958 and 1959, respectively.

Two other additions occurred in 1959. The first was the 501 Workmaster series of high-crop off-set cultivating tractors. The second was the Select-O-Speed power-shift planetary transmission providing ten speeds forward and two in reverse.

For all of its marketing effort in providing a multitude of models, Ford lost market share in 1956 and US production dropped below that of Ford, UK. This trend was to continue until the end of Fordson production in 1964. In some of these years, English production was triple that of American.

In 1959 the color scheme for the Workmaster line was changed to all red with gray trim. The Powermaster line continued the red cast iron and gray sheet metal, but added a red hood center strip and red grille.

In 1961, Ford took the first step in consolidating its worldwide tractor operations, which now also included an assembly plant in Brazil. The Tractor and Implement Division also introduced the first of the next generation of Ford tractors, the new Ford 6000. At the same time, worldwide trac-

Ford "Offset" tractors were built from 1958-1964. Nevertheless, they are very rare. Shown is a 1959 Model 501. After 1962 the model designation was 2111. These tractors were built especially for one-row cultivation.

tor activities were consolidated under a supervisory group called Ford Tractor Operations.

Collecting Comments

Although tractors in this section are all more than thirty years old, they lack so little in comparison to present-day machines that it is hard to consider them antiques. Except for a few, they are also readily available, and with no shortage of parts; factors leading to collector intrigue for other brands of this vintage. Therefore, the star ratings generally assume some waiting will be involved before the full potential of these Fords will be realized.

Because of all the models and variations possible with these tractors—ninety-three in all—the star ratings and model characteristics will be presented differently than in other chapters.

Early and late serial numbers are more in demand, of course. Accessories such as the Ford over/underdrive add value, as does an appropriate implement.

Characteristics
Basic Model Numbers
5—: One-row, 8in offset design equipped with 134ci gasoline, LPG, or 144ci four-cylinder diesel.

Palmer Fossum on his 1959 Model 501 Offset Workmaster. The 501 used the same 134ci engine as the earlier Models 600 and 700 except the compression ratio was increased from 6.6:1 to 7.5:1.

Just one easy step on or off

You don't need a stepladder with a FORD

Not a cent extra!

Power steering now standard on all new Ford Tricycles

Any farmer who has driven old-fashioned tricycle tractors knows what a man-saver power steering can be. On Ford's new Tricycle Tractors you can turn the wheel with one finger even when the tractor is stopped!

And best of all, with a Ford you don't have to dig down into your pocket to enjoy power steering. It's standard — not one red cent extra!

Another reason why FORD is first and far ahead in NEW DAY FARMING

One of the first things you'll notice when you try out a Ford Tractor is how much easier you can get on or off. Just one easy step and you're settled into the comfortable, low-mounted seat. You don't have to scramble over rear-attached implements or climb up to a hard-to-reach seat.

There are many more features in Ford Tractors that add to your comfort and safety . . . such as Rest-O-Ride seat, quiet muffler, Proof-Meter, safety starter, weatherproof ignition, and much more.

You get a bonus of power in the new Ford Tractors, too — up to 35 percent more power than previous models.

So see your nearby Ford Tractor and Implement Dealer. See how Ford Tractors and matched implements can make your farm work easier and more profitable. Tractor and Implement Division, Ford Motor Co., Birmingham, Michigan.

Ford Farming IS NEW DAY FARMING

Tricycle tractors were announced in 1956 as the 700 and 900 series. Power steering was standard equipment.

Power steering became an option for automobiles in 1952. By 1956, when this ad appeared, power steering was a popular option for tractors. On Ford tricycle models, it was standard equipment.

Russell Hanson, Ellison Bay, Wisconsin, bought this Jubilee new back in 1953. It was his third new Ford tractor; the other two being a 1942 2N and a 1948 8N. His dealer, George Rankin of Sturgeon Bay, Wisconsin, now 91 years old, remembers selling eighteen 8Ns in forty-five minutes. After he had assembled the prospects, he had demonstrated the ability of the 8N to plow up a steep hill in wet, heavy clay. After that he just sat down and wrote orders.

This 1961 Ford 971 LPG has not yet seen the touch of the restorer's hand, but it soon will. It is owned by restorer and collector Dwight Emstrom of Galesburg, Illinois. The LPG engine used an 8.65:1 compression ratio to fully obtain the benefits of this type of fuel.

Ford's low-priced tractor, the Model 630, was announced in 1956. The 630 was not equipped with a PTO.

This late 1957 ad shows the 861 Powermaster.
Note the fortieth anniversary icon, bottom center,
celebrating the history of mass-produced tractors.

Ford 501 Offsets are rare enough, but the diesel version is even more rare. This 1959 version is owned by collector Dwight Emstrom of Galesburg, Illinois, who bought it from a Florida watermelon grower. The one-row mounted cultivator is controlled by the three-point quadrant.

6—: Four-wheel utility type, with adjustable front axle. Equipped with 134ci gasoline, LPG, or 144ci diesel.

7—: High-clearance row-crop type equipped with 134ci gasoline, LPG, or 144ci four-cylinder diesel.

8—: Four-wheel utility type with adjustable front axle. Equipped with 172ci gasoline, LPG, or diesel engine.

9—: High-clearance row-crop type. Equipped with 172ci gasoline, LPG, or diesel engine.

Middle Number

-1-: Select-O-Speed transmission without PTO.

-2-: Four-speed transmission, no PTO or three-point hitch.

-3-: Four-speed transmission without PTO.

-4-: Four-speed transmission with PTO and three-point hitch.

-5-: Five-speed transmission, non-live PTO, three-point hitch.

-6-: Five-speed transmission, live PTO, three-point hitch.

-7-: Select-O-Speed transmission, single-speed PTO, three-point hitch.

-8-: Select-O-Speed transmission, with two-speed live and ground-drive (non-live) PTO. Three-point hitch.

Dash Numbers and Letters

___-1: Tricycle type with single front wheel (add one star).

___-4: High-clearance four-wheel adjustable (add one star).

___-L: LPG engine (add one star).

___-D: Diesel engine.

Serial Number

Year	Beginning Serial Number
600, 700, 800, 900 Series	
1964	1
1955	10615
1956	77615
1957	116368

NEWEST FORD DIESEL!

2-3 Plow Power

Owners Report:

Fuel costs only 10¢ per acre in heavy plowing!

NOW!

SELECT-O-SPEED

SELECT-O-SPEED
Shift to any Speed on the GO!

Cut your tractor expense to the bone! Now you can plow for approximately *half* the fuel cost of your gasoline tractor—reduce your tractor fuel bills up to 50% *and even more* on all kinds of farm work.

Best of all, new Ford 2-3 plow *diesel* tractors are in the same price range* as comparable gasoline tractors of other makes! So no longer must you pay a big pre-

mium to enjoy all the advantages of diesel power. Other advantages include low upkeep, few overhauls, extra lugging power.

So see them at your nearby Ford tractor dealer's. Ask about the other sizes of Ford-built diesel tractors—all best buys in their power class. Easy terms, too.

Based on F.O.B. factory suggested list prices of other make tractors, as published when this advertisement was prepared.

YOU GET A LOT MORE FOR A LOT LESS FROM

FORD

Select-O-Speed transmissions were not too common on the Workmaster line of tractors, but they were available. This ad shows an all-red (except for fenders and wheels) paint scheme.

Power steering, as indicated by the circular plate under the steering wheel nut, was standard equipment on Ford's row-crop tractors in 1957. Note the full-panel of gauges, too. Shown is a 1957 Model 960.

The draft control mechanism for Offset tractors requires some additional linkages.

Year	Beginning Serial Number
501, 601, 701, 801, 901 Series	
1957	1001
1958	11977
1959	58312
1960	105943
1961	155531

In 1956, Ford introduced its row-crop tractors. The 700 and 900 series were tricycle versions of the 600 and 800 models announced for 1955. The 700 was available as the Model 740, with a four-speed transmission. The 900 was available as the 950, with a five-speed transmission; and the 960 was available with a five-speed transmission and a live PTO. By the end of 1957, the tractors were given a face-lift and a 1 was added to the model designation. Shown here is a 1957 Model 960.

By 1957, the Series 700 and 900 tractors were available in dual tricycle, single front wheel, and wide-front row-crop styles. Additional clearance for the rear axle was obtained by adding a gear mesh at the end of each rear axle. Shown here is Dwight Emstrom's 1957 Model 960.

Operating the Hydraulics

There seems to be much confusion and misinformation about the proper operation of Fordson, Ford-Ferguson, and Ford tractor hydraulics. The following owner's manual excerpts are included to shed some light on the subject.

Draft Control

Where contour and soil conditions constantly change or when surface conditions are such that loss of traction can be expected, draft control enables work to be completed that would be impossible without it.

To engage draft control, position the Draft/Position lever under the seat to horizontal (for 8Ns, vertical for Fordson Dexta; 9Ns and 2Ns only have draft control; check owner's manual). Place the control lever at the bottom of the quadrant to lower the implement for

An eyewitness to history, 79-year-old Harold Brock holds the demonstration model of the tractor he designed. Brock started with Ford in 1929, graduated from the Henry Ford Trade School (a classmate of Robert McNamara's), and worked intimately with both Ford and Ferguson as project leader and designer of the 9N and subsequent tractors up to 1959. The spring-wound model propelled itself along the track until the plow struck an obstacle. With the three-point plow as shown, the tractor stalled; with a conventional trailing plow (not shown) striking the obstacle caused the tractor to rear.

work, then raise the lever until the desired working depth is reached. The lower the lever is placed on the quadrant, the greater the working depth will be.

The implement now operates at this depth as long as draft remains constant, but if a heavy patch of soil or an obstruction is encountered, the hydraulic system will respond by raising the implement. Likewise, if the front wheels cross a ridge, the implement tends to go deeper into the soil. As it does, increased draft compresses the draft spring and moves the internal lift control. The implement raises until the ridge is passed. Then the lessening draft is overcome by the spring and the implement is returned automatically to its previous depth.

For heavy operations, such as plowing, connect the top link to the lowest hole in the draft control rocker. (Dextas have two holes; most 8Ns have three holes; 9Ns, 2Ns, and the rest of the 8Ns only have one hole.) For light draft operations, such as cultivating, make the connection to the top hole.

In light soil never operate with the main control lever against the bottom of the quadrant as the implement may go to uncontrolled maximum depth and damage the hydraulics.

Position Control

This control allows the operator to set an implement at any required position relative to the tractor, and this will automatically be maintained irrespective of changes in soil resistance. This is particularly suitable where the ground is level and soil conditions consistent. It is also to be used for mowers and sprayers.

Adjustable Control Lever Stop

Once the desired work depth has been obtained, the adjustable stop on the quadrant may be set to contact the main control lever. After any cycle of operations the implement can be returned to the same working position by moving the control lever to the stop.

Hy-Trol (For tractors after 1953)

Regardless of where the Hy-Trol control is set, it does not affect the rate of operation with the main quadrant control, but only that of the draft control spring linkage. When plowing, for instance, greater flow is needed for the first run of openings. This enables the maximum benefit to be obtained from a rapid number of weight transfer reactions. Under normal conditions, better quality of work can be obtained by using a reduced setting.

Raising For Transport

Lift the control lever until it is at the top of the quadrant and the implement will be lifted to the fully raised position. Here it will remain until the quadrant lever is again placed in the lower position. Under position control, any height less than fully raised may be obtained by raising the quadrant lever a corresponding amount. Under draft control, however, intermediate heights may only be obtained by first raising the lever to the top of the quadrant and then moving it downward when the implement reaches the desired height. This movement is comparatively small and is required to neutralize the internal linkage.

The Powermaster line is advertised as a four-plow tractor in 1959.

Chapter 7

Ford Tractors, Blue and White— Models 2000 through 6000

In March 1961, Ford's Whiz Kid management established Ford Tractor Operations to coordinate the domestic activities of the Tractor and Implement Division with those of Ford Motor Company Limited. This was the first step in the plan to make a more consistent line of tractors for worldwide distribution, eliminating competition between US- and UK-built tractors. Later in the year, the new six-cylinder Model 6000 was introduced. At about the same time, the model designations of the industrial line of tractors was changed to be consistent with the new 6000. The Model 4000 replaced the 801 and the 2000 replaced the 601. The color scheme for industrial models was changed to red-trimmed yellow.

In early 1962, the name "Ford Tractor Operations" was changed to the Ford Tractor Division. The numbers of the agricultural tractors were all changed that year to the four-digit scheme. The Fordson Super Major was given the Ford 5000 designation while the Super Dexta was called the Ford 2000 Diesel. This was a stopgap measure to carry them over until the "World" tractors could be readied. The paint combinations were also changed so that all tractors were painted in variations of blue and gray, rather than red and gray (domestic) and blue and orange (UK).

Post-1965 Models

Since these last models discussed are still so

Basic Model Number	Offset 2000	Reg. 2000	R-crop 2000	Reg. 4000	R-crop 4000	Ind. 2000	Ind. 4000	6000
S-O-S trans., no PTO	★★★	★★	★★★	★★	★★	★★	★★	
4-speed, no PTO or hyd.	★★	★	★★	★	★	★	★	
4-speed, no PTO	★★	★	★★	★	★	★★	★★	
4-speed, PTO and hyd.	★★★★	★★	★★★	★★	★★	★★	★★	
5-speed, non-live PTO	★★★★	★★	★★★	★★	★★	★★	★★	
5-speed, live PTO	★★★★	★★★	★★★★	★★★	★★★	★★	★★	
S-O-S, 1 speed. PTO	★★★★	★★★	★★★★	★★★	★★★	★★	★★	
S-O-S, full-up PTO	★★★★	★★★	★★★★	★★★★	★★★★	★★	★★★	★★★

★★	Model 2000
★★★	Model 3000
★★	Model 4000
★★★	Model 5000
★★★	Model 6000

A 1967 Ford 4000 Diesel tractor at work in Kelly's Farm Market orchard near Rochester, Minnesota. The 4000 was rated at 45.71 PTO horsepower. It used a 201ci three-cylinder engine. It's carrying a three-point PTO sprayer.

new, they are not generally considered collectible. Some of the more prominent collectors are beginning to add them, however. The following star ratings are assigned with an eye to the future and are so general that credit for detail model variation is not given. The Ford tractor enthusiast will have to make his own adjustments as time goes on, taking into account personal preferences.

Ford's World Tractor Operation

In 1964, thirty-one years of tractor production ended at Dagenham and with it came the end of the Fordson name. A new tractor plant was opened in Basildon, England. Concurrently, the Tractor Division converted the Antwerp, Belgium, plant to tractor production. Incidentally, tractor production in Dagenham's last year was more than double that of US-built (now at Highland Park) tractors.

Highland Park's production of a few more than 25,000 would hardly have excited Old Henry Ford, had he lived to be 100. For all their management techniques and model variations, the Whiz Kids hadn't come close to equaling the domestic production of the single-model days.

Late in 1964, the new worldwide line of Ford tractors was announced for the 1965 model year. Completely new tractors replaced the previous 2000-5000 series. Row-crop and offset tractors were eliminated from the line (except for the row-crop 6000). Innovative new three-cylinder engines replaced the four-cylinder units in the 2000-4000 series. The Model 5000 got a four-cylinder derivation of the new engine, while the 6000 was essentially unchanged except for its designation now as the Commander 6000.

The new tractors were much more like the

The Ford Tractor Division of the Ford Motor Company was established in 1962. Previously called Ford Tractor and Implement Operations, a worldwide product consolidation program was begun in 1960. New color schemes and new model designations were instituted for both US- and British-made tractors. Shown here is Palmer Fossum's 1962 Model 4000 Industrial. It is presently awaiting restoration and repainting to its original buff and blue colors.

The non-adjustable front axle used on Ford industrial and orchard tractors in the sixties.

Dexta and Super Major than they were like Jubilee derivatives. In fact, outside the United States the 2000 was known as the Dexta 2000 and the 5000 was called the Super Major 5000.

The "new" Commander 6000 was not much like the World tractors. It was only marketed in the United States, Canada, and Australia. It was available in both row-crop and all-purpose models with gas, LPG, or diesel engines.

In 1966, the Ford Tractor Division entered a new marketplace. They began marketing a line of lawn and garden equipment manufactured for them by Jacobsen. Industrial versions of the agricultural tractors had "500" added to the model number; i.e., 3500, 4500, etc.

By 1966, Ford tractor production brought the company to the number two position in the world. The number one company worldwide was Massey Ferguson, the company derived from Massey-Har-

A 1972 Ford Roadmower Special owned by the Rockford (Illinois) Airport Authority. Operator Nick Duffy drives this machine about forty hours per week every summer mowing the airport perimeter. This 2110 model was built from 1968-1975.

The Roadmower has extended rear axles for hillside stability. Also note the foot throttle by the running board.

The 1972 Ford Roadmower owned by the Rockford (Illinois) Airport Authority has over 8,000 hours on the tach. According to the operator Nick Duffy, it has not had any major work on its three-cylinder engine.

The Model 4000 Industrial utilized the ten-speed Select-O-Speed planetary transmission. The quadrant control was lighted for easy reading at night.

ris and Ferguson. After the merger, Harry Ferguson receded from the tractor business and died in 1960, but wouldn't he have enjoyed seeing Ford play catch-up?

Epilogue

The Ford Tractor Division celebrated its sixtieth anniversary in 1977 by entering the super-tractor realm. A family of four-wheel drive articulated tractors was announced. These monsters were made for Ford by Steiger Tractor Company.

To posture itself in the worldwide implement business, Ford purchased the New Holland Company in 1987. Also in 1987, the company purchased the Canadian Versatile Tractor Company.

In 1991, the New Holland Holding Company was formed. The assets of Ford-New Holland and Fiat Agri were placed under its control. Ford

The Ford 4000 replaced the 901 in 1962. This one is equipped with the optional Select-O-Speed power shift transmission.

This 1968 Ford 3400 Industrial seems to have non-standard rear fenders. Flat-top fenders were available on some 1975 models.

owned 20 percent of the holding company and Fiat owned 80 percent. In 1992, Fiat, through a $600 million infusion of cash, increased its share to 88 percent.

Collecting Comments

Since the pre- and post-1965 tractors are so different, they will be treated separately. Pre-1965 tractors are essentially the same as the Workmaster-Powermaster tractors of 1958-1961, except for paint and model number changes.

Characteristics:

Agricultural and industrial model numbers consist of five digits, in some cases followed by a letter or a number. The following list shows how it works out.

2—— Indicates a 134ci gas engine or a 144ci diesel
4—— Indicates a 172ci gas, LPG, or diesel engine
-0— Industrial models prior to 1963
-1— Industrial and agricultural models after 1963
—10- Row crop
—11- Offset
—20- Utility type, adjustable front axle
—21- Orchard type, non-adjustable front axle. Add one star
—31- Low center of gravity (LCG) type. Add one star
—41- Heavy-duty industrial, stub frame/cast grille
-1—0 Four-speed, no PTO
-0—1 Four-speed, no PTO or hydraulics
-1—1 Four-speed with PTO
-0—2 Four-speed with hydraulics, no PTO

NEW! FORD 6000

Never Before a 5-Plow Tractor with All These Advanced Features!

- A hydraulic system, for example, that stores hydraulic power for instant peak-load use. *Only Ford has it!*
- A power-shift transmission that lets you shift to any gear on-the-go, under full load. *Only Ford has it!*
- Two-position steering wheel for both sit-down and stand-up driving. *Only Ford has it!*
- Power take-off that delivers standard PTO speeds at two different throttle settings, for both light and heavy PTO work. *Only Ford has it!*

All this plus hydraulic power brakes, power steering, power adjusted rear wheels. Smooth 6-cylinder gasoline or diesel engines. Big matched equipment. *Ford Motor Company,*

New! Only Ford tractors have on-the-go shifting to any speed at any time. Just moving the gear selector lever does it! Ten speeds forward, two in reverse. Ford Select-O-Speed has been proved by over a million hours of operation.

New! Power brakes, disc type, oil cushioned. Always in balance, with equalized braking pressure for safe, sure stops. Never need adjusting. Sealed from water, dust and dirt. Smooth and responsive—light pedal pressure for easier control.

New! Quick-adjustable steering wheel. The steering wheel raises and swings forward for stand-up driving; lowers and swings rearward for sit-down driving. This, with power steering, gives the easiest steering ever. Just feel the difference!

The Model 6000, although not one of Ford's most popular tractors, was quite advanced for its time. This 1961 advertisement lists some of its unique features.

142

A 1968 Model 3000 in very nice original condition.

A rather rare 1960 Model 4040 (Ford 4000 Industrial) is shown here with a front end loader.

-1—2 Five-speed with live PTO
-0—3 Four-speed with hydraulics and PTO
-0—4 Select-O-Speed without hydraulics or PTO
-1—4 Select-O-Speed without PTO
-0—5 Select-O-Speed with hydraulics and 540rpm PTO
-0—6 Select-O-Speed with hydraulics, 540rpm and 1000rpm, and ground speed PTO
-1—6 Select-O-Speed with 540rpm and 1000rpm independent PTO
-1—7 Select-O-Speed with 540rpm and 1000rpm independent and ground speed PTO

Suffix letters and numbers signify the following:
-1 Tricycle type with a single front wheel
-4 High-clearance, four-wheel, adjustable front axle

-D Diesel engine
-L LPG engine

Serial Number

Year	Beginning Serial Number
2000 and 4000 series	
1962	1001
1963	11949
1964	38931
6000 Series	
1961	131591
1962	171542
1962 (Blue line)	1001
1963	11948
1964	38931

A 1963 Ford 2000 Offset. Actually, the complete model number is 2111, indicating a 134ci engine, offset configuration, and four-speed transmission with PTO.

144

Dwight Emstrom's 1968 Ford 3000 is, he says, his favorite tractor. The three-cylinder engine is as smooth as a six. Weighing in at about 4,000lb, it has plenty of beef for most jobs.

Serial Number

Year	Beginning Serial Number
2000, 3000 and 4000 Series	
1965	C100000
1966	C123000
1967	C160000
1968	C188000
Commander 6000 Series	
1965	C100000
1966	C123000
1967	C160000

The Ford 2000 Offset is essentially the same as the 1959 501 Workmaster Offset. The engine is off-set to the left, while the driver's seat is offset to the right. This provides the operator with unobstructed vision for monitoring the one-row cultivator.

The Ford 3000 has a three-cylinder 158ci engine rated at 38 PTO horsepower. The diesel version of this tractor used a 175ci engine. Owner Dwight Emstrom is shown on the tractor.

Although not the prettiest specimen, this was the only Ford 6000 tractor the author was able to find, indicating a certain amount of rarity. The 6000 was produced between 1961-1967 and sold in the United States, Canada, and Australia.

The Ford 6000 was available in gasoline, LPG, and diesel versions of the six-cylinder engine. The gasoline and LPG engines displaced 223ci, while the diesel, as shown here, displaced 242ci.

This particular Ford 6000 had just been sold for $2,000. Not bad for a thirty-year-old tractor in *au naturel* condition.

Chapter 8

Specifications and Data

About 1915, a Nebraska farmer named Wilmot F. Crozier, who had also been a schoolteacher (to support the farm, he said), purchased a "Ford" tractor from the Minneapolis outfit not related to Henry Ford. (They had a man named Ford join the company in order to use the name.) The tractor was so unsatisfactory that he demanded the company replace it. They did, but the replacement was worse. Farmer Crozier then bought a Bull tractor. This too was completely unsatisfactory. Next, he bought a 1918 Rumely "Three-plow." The Rumely met and exceeded Crozier's expectations. Not only did it stand up to the strains of farming, he was able to regularly pull a five-bottom plow. Shortly afterward, Crozier was elected to the Nebraska legislature.

In 1919, Representative Crozier and Senator Charles Warner introduced legislation that result-ed in the Nebraska Test Law. The law required that any tractor sold in the state of Nebraska had to be certified by the state. The state was to test the tractors to see that they lived up to their advertised claims. The University of Nebraska's Agricultural Engineering Department would conduct the tests. L. W. Chase and Claude Shedd devised the tests and the test equipment, which have since become standards for the world.

The first test was made in the fall of 1919 (things happened a lot faster in those days) of a Twin City 12-20, but could not be completed because of snowfall. The first complete test was made in the spring of 1920. A certificate was issued for the Waterloo Boy Model N.

The results of tests of Ford tractors made between 1918 and 1957 follow.

Ford Nebraska Tractor Tests Summary

Model Year	Test Number	Fuel	Max. HP Belt/PTO	Max. HP Drawbar	Max. Pull	Fuel cons.	Weight	Wheels
Fordson 1920	18	K	18.2	9.34	2187	7.32	2710	S
Fordson 1926	124	K	22.3	12.3		9.63	3175	S
Fordson 1930 Type N	173	K	23.2	13.6	3289	7.07	3820	S
Fordson 1930 Type N	174	Gas	29.1	15.5		9.53	3800	S
9N 1940	339	Gas	23.1	12.8	2236	9.74	3677	R
8N 1950	443	Ga.	25.5	20.8	2810	11.2	4043	R
Jubilee 1953	494	Ga.	32.4	26.8	3232	11.2	4389	R
Major 1953	500	D	38.5	34.2	5315	15.5	7890	R
660 1955	561	Gas	35.2	29.8	3859	11.3	4917	R
851 1958	640	Gas	50.2	43.28	5033	11.7	6855	R
851 1958	654	D	44.5	38.9	5120	14.4	6885	R
641 1959	686	D	31.8	28.5	4230	15.0	5897	R
6000 1961	784	G	66.9	59.4		10.4	9535	R
S Dexta 1963	844	D	38.8	32.3		15.5	6030	R
3000 1965	881	D	39.2	34.9		16.8	6885	R
5000 1966	932	Gas	60.4	50.9		11.9	9650	R
2000 1967	959	Gas	31.2	27.5		16.0	5860	R

Notes on Nebraska Tractor Tests

Fuel: K = Kerosene; Gas. = Gasoline; D = Diesel; LPG = Liquefied Petroleum Gas, or propane

Belt/PTO Horsepower: This is Test C horsepower, maximum attainable at the PTO or belt pulley. If the generator, hydraulic pump, etc., were not standard equipment, they were removed for these tests.

Drawbar Horsepower: Taken from Test G data, it is based on maximum drawbar pull and speed. The difference between this and PTO HP is due to slippage, and to the power required to move the tractor itself. The heavier the tractor, the less the slippage, but the more power required to move the tractor. Factory engineers looked for the ideal compromise.

Max. Pull: Test G.

Fuel Cons.: The rate of fuel consumption in horsepower hours per gallon.

Weight: The weight of the tractor plus ballast in pounds. Ballast was often added for Test G and other heavy pulling tests, and then removed for other tests to improve performance.

Wheels: S = Steel; R = Rubber

Ford Tractor Specifications

Model	Years (19—)	Bore/ Stroke	No. of cyl.	Disp.	Rated RPM	Forward Speeds	Basic Weight	Fuel
Fordson	18-27	4.00x5.00	4	251	1100	3	2700	K
Fordson	33-46	4.12x5.00	4	267	1100	3	3600	K
E27N	46-53	4.12x5.00	4	267	1200	3	4000	K
9N	39-42	3.19x3.75	4	119.7	2000	3	2340	G
8N	47-52	3.19x3.75	4	119.7	200	4	2410	G
Major	53-58	3.74x4.52	4	199	1600	6	5100	*
P Major	58-60	3.94x4.52	4	220	1600	6	5300	D
S Major	61-64	3.94x4.52	4	220	1700	6	5300	D
Dexta	58-61	3.50x5.00	3	144	2000	6	3000	D
S Dexta	62-64	3.60x5.00	3	153	2250	6	3000	D
Jubilee	63-64	3.44x3.60	4	134	2000	4	2510	G
601	59-61	3.56x3.60	4	144	2000	4/5/10	3375	D
800	54-61	3.90x3.60	4	172	2000	4/5/10	3450	*
2000	65-68	4.20x3.80	3	158	2000	4/8	4000	*
3000	65-68	4.20x4.20	3	175	2000	8/10	4100	*
4000	65-68	4.40x4.20	3	192	2200	8/10	4770	G
4000	65-68	4.40x4.40	3	201	2200	8/10	4900	D
5000	65-68	4.23x4.20	4	233	2100	8/10	5830	*
6000	61-67	3.62x3.60	6	223	2300	10	7000	G
6000	61-67	3.62x3.90	6	242	2230	10	7165	D

* Available in gasoline, LPG, and/or diesel

Chapter 9

How to Buy a Collector Tractor

If you already have your tractor, you won't have to face the choosing and buying problems; you've already been through that at least once. If, however, you don't have one but have decided which model you want, then the acquisition is the next phase. The checklist included in this chapter will help you organize your thoughts and arrive at a fair price for the tractor.

The first decision you should make is the level of restoration you want to tackle. Are you into a 100 percent original restoration? Do you just want a nice old tractor around to help you in gardening and making firewood? Or do you want something in between?

Understand that those who are into originality go all the way. Originality means not using modern-tread tires. It means using wiring, hose clamps, spark plugs, and tire valve caps from the tractor's era. It means being a stickler for details most people wouldn't notice. This level of restoration is essential to realize the potential value of a four- or five-star tractor. If you have a run-of-the-mill tractor, then maybe something less than as-original will suffice. The sad part is that a true five-star machine is not good for anything but display and an occasional parade. I find that people with such tractors have at least one other one of lesser value for work and fun.

Next, you need to decide whether you want to buy a tractor that's already been restored, one you can restore completely by yourself, or one where you will get expert help in the process. Whichever course you take, it is essential that you clearly define your objectives for class rating and cost.

Where do you look for a collectible Ford-built tractor? The first place, for an N or later tractor, is the Farm Equipment section in the classified ads of your local newspaper. For the old Fordsons, or

anything unusual, try other collectors, an ad placed in the *9N-2N-8N Newsletter*, or the antique tractor line up at your local thresheree and steam show. Your local Ford tractor dealer is also usually a good source. The dealer will often have an N or Dexta on the used tractor row.

I recently answered the following ad from my local newspaper:

Ford 800 tractor with three-point disk, blade and Woods mower. Good condition. Call XXX-XXXX.

I called the number and the owner's wife answered. She said the tractor was in excellent shape, her husband wouldn't have it any other way, and that it had just been repainted. I got directions and went to see it.

It had indeed been repainted—right over the old decals. Oil was dripping from under the front of the engine, the muffler and exhaust were shot, the front tires were car snow tires, and the entire hood was loose enough to move around as the tractor was driven.

The reason I include this story is to point out how disappointing the search for the tractor you want can be—the high expectations of the search can be followed by the dashed hopes of finding a Class 5 when you expected a Class 3. Not to be discouraged, however, there are two important questions to ask yourself: Is the price fair? Do I want to get involved in the amount of work required to put the tractor into the shape I want?

To help you determine the fairness of the price, and to systematically determine how much work and cost you would be facing, the following buyer's checklist is included. For best results, customize the checklist for the type of tractor you are looking for and the type of work you are willing to undertake.

Take your checklist with you when you evaluate a tractor for purchase. Check the items off as they appear on the list, making notes on each section as you go. The purpose of this is twofold. First, using a checklist is an orderly way to complete the evaluation with as much rationality as possible. Second, keeping a record of the evaluation will let you compare it to others, allowing you to get a handle on the fairness of the price. If you are going to hire out some or all of the work, your notes on the checklist will help the mechanic give you a cost estimate.

Checklist

General Appearance
Sheet metal—grill; fenders
Tires—wheels
Gauges—correct; operable
Seat—correct; condition
Exhaust
Oil; water—fuel leaks
Model designation
Serial number
Ask what is included (wheel weights, implements, etc.)

Steering
Steering wheel free play
Kingpin free play
Radius rod free play
Front wheel bearing free play
Drag arm(s) free play
Steering wheel condition

Before Starting Engine
Water pump or generator shaft end play
Belt pulley end play
Evidence of crack repair, block—head
Oil in crankcase
Filter in place
Water in crankcase
Water in radiator
Oil in water
Belts
Hoses
Radiator cap
Air cleaner
Carburetor—injector controls
Fuel tank—fuel in tank
Fuel filter—sediment bowl; shut-off turned on

Electrical
Battery in place—condition; water
Battery box—corrosion
Magneto—coils
Cables—terminals
Generator—brushes
Starter—visible condition

Key/Switch—location; operation
Diesel shut-off operational
Ammeter indication—key on and off
Plug wire condition
General wiring condition
Lights

Clutch/Transmission
Clutch operation
Shift lever operation
Oil level
Water in oil
Leaks; welds; repairs
Shift lever boot (if so equipped)

Rear Axle
Housing cracks; repairs; leaks
Lubricant level—water present?
Axle wheel seals
Brakes/lining—linkage

After Starting Engine
Oil pressure
Smoke/tailpipe—breather
Knocking
Miss
Temperature stabilizes
Throttle response rpm range—governor operation
Oil; water; hydraulics—leaks
Starter operation
Generator charging

Clutch/Transmission
Clutch releases completely
Gear selection
Clutch engages smoothly
Clutch slippage
Free pedal
PTO operation
Differential lock operation

Brakes
Left and right brake power

Hydraulic System
Lift ability
Leak down
Smoothness

Road—Field Test
Steering shimmy—binding
Brakes
Engine operation under load
Hydraulics operation
Water temperature
Inappropriate noises

Comments on the General Checklist

General Appearance

Rust and corrosion indicate outdoor storage for long periods, which can ruin internal parts as well. Look for extraneous holes or modifications to the sheet metal and fenders. Some of these parts can be expensive to replace if not repairable. Be aware of the many aluminum castings used on early 9Ns. These may have been broken and replaced by later cast iron parts (a no-no for four- or five-star restorations). Check for proper sheet metal fasteners. If you are going for four- or five-star restoration, visible fasteners must be of the original type. If the paint job is recent, is it good enough for you? Are the decals proper? If not, you will be asked to pay for something you can't use.

Model Designation and Serial Number

These are included so that proper credit will be given if the tractor is historically significant or rare. Lack of definite evidence of model or serial number can impede the acquisition of parts, and may be evidence that the configuration is not original. Generally, the serial number is the only "hard data" on the bill of sale by which to identify the tractor. With many of the Ford-built tractors, the serial number is on the engine. If the engine has been changed, all historical bets are off. You have to know if the rest of the tractor lines up with the engine number.

Tires and Wheels

Do they match, left and right? Are the tires weather checked? Hairline cracks are acceptable, but major cracks will cause trouble. Splits and cracks can indicate the existence of a boot or tire liner. These are okay, but reduce the value. With a new set of current-production tires costing between $600-$1,000, their condition vitally affects the value of the tractor. Obtaining good tires with tread appropriate to the year of the tractor can be difficult and even more costly.

Wheels also bear close inspection. Check for corrosion from farm chemicals and tire fluid. Check the wheel-mounting holes for cracks or elongation. Check the wheels for wobble, which could mean a bent rim or axle.

Steel wheels are an even bigger "watch-out." Steel wheels do not necessarily have to be of the type that came with the tractor, but must be appropriate for the time frame.

Steering

Steering wheel free play of about 45 degrees is the limit of acceptability for more or less "modern" tractors. Up to 90 degrees can be tolerated on a Fordson F, N, or E27N. Determine where the looseness is, however, as it may be an indication of needed expensive repairs.

Grasp the tops of the front wheels and try to move them in and out. Looseness and clunking are an indication of kingpin and/or wheel bearing play. Check the steering wheel itself in the same way to see if all the bearings are sound.

Before Starting

It is important that these tests be done before attempting to start the engine, unless the tractor has been recently run. Not only will this prevent damage from things like lack of oil, but it will also allow you to check for water in the oil, or oil in the water, before operation gets everything mixed up. It will, in addition, serve as a setup check, so you don't, for example, attempt to start the engine with the fuel shut off.

Engine

As you make these checks, make the engine ready to start. That is, open the fuel shut-off, add oil, fuel, and water as necessary. If the engine is inoperable, do your best to determine why. Is there compression? Is there spark? Is the fuel getting through? Is the engine "stuck"? A truly stuck engine is a problem, but is not insurmountable.

Engines can almost always be "unstuck" by pressure—hydraulic pressure. The ultimate way to free an engine is to take it to a machine shop and have the pistons pressed out. Before getting to that point, though, you should try to soak it free by filling the cylinders, through the spark plug holes, with a penetrating oil (don't put the plugs back in, except very loosely). Periodically, give it a try with the hand crank or with the jacked-up back wheel (which can go back or forth). There are many ways to proceed if you find a stuck engine, but the point here is to correctly evaluate what you are up against and proceed accordingly.

Electrical

The ammeter indication item is intended to show that the ignition system and switch are functional by observing an indication of "discharge" when the switch is turned on. When checking the lights, see if they are genuine Ford items or aftermarket parts. A four- or five-star restoration must have "the right stuff."

Clutch/Transmission

It is important to ascertain that the clutch is actually released when the pedal is in the "release" position, and/or that the transmission is actually in neutral, before attempting to manually start the engine. Failure to do so could result in your being run over!

Hydraulics

It's best to check the hydraulics with a heavy implement such as a plow or mower deck. The system should be able to raise and hold anything designed for it with ample reserve. With the engine off, the system should not let the implement down for at least ten minutes.

Road-Field Test

Ideally, operate the tractor in a field with an implement such as a plow or mower. You should also take it where you can operate it at top road speed. Try all the gears and the brakes. Operate it long enough for things to get warm. Listen for any unusual sounds as it warms up.

Summary

Again, remember that the point of these tests is not so much to accept or reject the tractor, but to determine if the price is fair and if you are prepared for the level of work needed. Some get their enjoyment from actually doing the work of bringing a Class 5 up to a Class 1. Others like to do the mechanical work and have specialists complete the painting and finishing. Personally, I'd rather buy a Class 1 or 2 and spend my time writing books.

Buying the Tractor

When considering the purchase of a tractor located some distance from your base of operations, get as much information on its condition as you can before making the trip. You might consider sending the checklist to the owner and asking him to fill it out and return it. Ask him to send along some pictures, too. Even with precautions, don't be surprised if things are not all that you expected.

It is best to have a price in mind when you first contact a prospective seller; but it is up to the seller to quote his asking price first. The same is true of auctions; have your upper-limit dollar figure firmly in mind before the bidding starts. With the individual seller, you usually start at his price and bargain downward; with the auction, it's the opposite. If you find you are too far apart, tell the seller how you arrived at your figure (based on similar sales, advertisements, or estimated value upon completion). Then give him your name and phone number on paper and leave. If your facts are convincing, he may come around. You won't likely cause him to change his price a lot, however, unless he has time to check out your logic.

Don't overlook the opportunity for barter in the transaction. Perhaps you have something to trade, or can provide some type of professional ser-

vice for the seller. Also, look for things to be "thrown in" on the deal. For example, the seller may be able to transport the tractor home for you, or you may require that he do some work on it before you take it away.

Once you've struck a deal, you'll be expected to come up with an acceptable form of payment (assuming it wasn't a complete barter deal). If you are close to home, matters are simplified: Write a check for the amount, wait for the check to clear, and then pick up your tractor. If waiting is not acceptable, you'll need cash, a certified check, or traveler's checks. Unless you have already agreed upon a price, the certified check will not likely be for the right amount. Make it out for your initial offer amount, then add to it with cash or traveler's checks to bring the amount up to the agreed upon price. If the amount of the transaction is small, or if the difference is not too great, some sellers may accept a personal check for the difference.

Tractors are unlike automobiles in that they do not have officially registered titles. How do you know, or how can you find out, if the person you are bargaining with really owns the tractor he is trying to sell you? One of the first things you should ask the seller is how long he has had the tractor and where he got it from. It's a good thing to ask, at that point, if he still has the bill of sale. If he doesn't, and has not had the tractor long, he should be willing to go back to the previous owner to get one. If he claims to be the original owner of a 50-year-old tractor and has no purchasing paperwork, you'll have to use your best judgment.

Be sure when you get your bill of sale that it includes the correct serial number or other identification. If the dollar amount is very large, or if you are uneasy about the legality of the sale, you might require notarization of the bill. At least you will have some recourse, if after you've completed the restoration, you find out you have to give the tractor back.

Once the money has changed hands, and you've gotten the bill of sale, you are the owner. Ordinarily, your homeowner's insurance will be sufficient protection for liabilities during restoration. If you are restoring tractors as a business, check with your insurance agent. If you transport the tractor home yourself, your regular truck or trailer insurance should apply to cargo. If the value of your purchase is great, you might be wise to talk to your agent about special coverage for it while in transit and while under restoration.

On the way home with your tractor, there are some things you may want to get done. You may want to take it to a place that has an engine degreasing service and have the whole tractor done. Assuming you have already done your best to operate the tractor to determine its condition, you may want to stop at a service station and have the oil, fuel, antifreeze, and tire liquid removed. You can, of course, remove these items in your own shop and then take them to a disposal facility, if you choose, but for most of us, this can be a messy procedure.

Collection Protection

Two-Cylinder, the official publication of Two-Cylinder Clubs, Worldwide, is a magazine for John Deere enthusiasts. A recent issue featured an article by Craig Beek, John Deere's manager for corporate security. Beek's article provides insights to help keep the antique tractor collector from being victimized by the unscrupulous. It is paraphrased here for the benefit of the Ford and Fordson collector.

As more people get into tractor collecting, as collector tractors become more difficult to find, and especially as values soar, the potential for fraud and theft also increases dramatically. Protect yourself during the buying process by getting and keeping plenty of proof of the transaction. Sometimes deals that sound too good to be true are just that.

Check and record the serial number. If the number is on a plate, examine it to see if it looks newer than the tractor. Does it look as if it has recently been installed? Engine block serial number stampings were often done by hand, and can look suspicious. See if you can detect stamp-overs, newly stamped, or uneven-sized numbers. In most states it is a felony to alter a factory-installed identification number. If an unscrupulous seller sees you are suspicious, when you ask for a notarized bill of sale with fingerprints, he's likely to start backing out of the sale.

Serial numbers aren't the only thing to watch out for. Let's say you are buying a low serial 9N with an aluminum hood and grille. It is a good idea to be able to trace the history of the rare hood and grille. Did they come with the tractor, are they reproductions, or did they come from a tractor that was scrapped out? If the latter is the case, it's best to determine that the scrapped tractor wasn't "chopped" by a thief. In such a case, get notarized documentation as to the legitimate sources of valuable parts.

The best advice to prevent being swindled is to create a paper trail with all important documents notarized. If, despite the precautions, you buy a stolen tractor, you lose. Law enforcement officials and the courts usually hold that a thief can pass no better title than he holds. At least your "black on white" will show you bought the machine in good faith.

Not only can the buyer be swindled by thieves, but he or she can be caught in the crossfire between feuding heirs disputing who has the rights to Grandpa's tractor. The heirs may think it's just a pile of junk. When the sale amounts to thousands of dollars, they can then change their minds.

After you have taken possession of the tractor, one of the best things you can do is take photographs or videos of it from every angle. Include the serial number plate or stamping and valuable parts, like new tires. You might also want to scribe your drivers license number or social security number in inconspicuous places. There is also a numbering system called the Iowa System.

With the Iowa System, your local sheriff assigns you an Owner Applied Identification Number (OAN) based on your state, county, and your name. The OAN is die-stamped somewhere on the tractor. When the tractor is sold, the new owner die-stamps his or her number below yours. Imagine that your tractor is stolen. You will want all the data and identification possible to give to the police! If your tractor is stolen, the investigating officer can enter the data in the FBI's National Crime Information Center (NCIC) computer. This computer serves as a link between law enforcement agencies.

Finally, make sure your insurance company knows about the tractor, especially if it is other than run of the mill. They should handle it just like any other valuable antique.

Should all this put a damper on your desire to get into collecting? Not at all. Just exercise proper precautions. On the whole, antique tractor people are by nature the absolute nicest people you are likely to run across and the unscrupulous are very few and far between.

Sources of Information and Help for the Collector

Books

The following books offer essential background on the tractors covered in this book. These make good reading and library additions for any tractor buff. Most are available from Motorbooks International Publishers & Wholesalers, P.O. Box 2, 729 Prospect Avenue, Osceola, WI 54020 USA.

The Agricultural Tractor 1855-1950, by R. B. Gray, Society of Agricultural Engineers. An outstanding and complete photo history of the origin and development of the tractor.

The American Farm Tractor, by Randy Leffingwell, Motorbooks International. A full-color hardcover history of all the great American tractor makes.

The American Ford, by Lorin Sorensen, Motorbooks International (reprint). A word and picture story of Henry Ford, his company, and its products.

The Century of the Reaper, by Cyrus McCormick, Houghton Mifflin Company. A firsthand account of the Harvester and Tractor Wars by the grandson of the inventor.

The Development of American Agriculture, by Willard W. Cochrane, University of Minnesota Press. An analytical history.

Farm Tractors 1926-1956, Randy Stephens, Editor, Intertec Publishing. A compilation of pages from *The Cooperative Tractor Catalog* and the *Red Tractor Book*.

Ford and Fordson Tractors, by Michael Williams, Blandford Press. A history of Henry Ford and his tractors, concentrating on the Fordson.

Ford Tractors, by Robert N. Pripps and Andrew Morland, Motorbooks International. A full-color history of the Fordson, Ford-Ferguson, Ferguson, and Ford tractors, covering the influence these historic tractors had on state-of-the-art of tractor design.

Ford Trucks Since 1905, by James K. Wagner, Crestline Publishing Company.

Fordson, Farmall and Poppin' Johnny, by Robert C. Williams, University of Illinois Press. A history of the farm tractor and its impact on America.

Harvest Triumphant, by Merrill Denison, Wm. Collins Sons & Company Ltd. The story of human achievement in the development of agricultural tools, especially in Canada, and the rise to prominence of Massey-Harris Ferguson (now known as the Verity Corporation). Rich in the romance of farm life in the last century and covering the early days of the Industrial Revolution.

How to Restore Your Farm Tractor, by Robert N. Pripps, Motorbooks International. Follows two tractors through professional restoration, one a 1939 Ford-Ferguson. Includes tips and techniques, commentary, and photos.

150 Years of International Harvester, by C. H. Wendel, Crestline Publishing. A complete photo-documented product history of International Harvester.

Threshers, by Robert N. Pripps and Andrew Morland, Motorbooks International. A color history of grain harvesting and threshing featuring photos and descriptions of many of the big threshers in operation.

Young Henry Ford, by Sidney Olson, Wayne State University Press. A pictorial history of Ford's first forty years.

Other Interesting Publications

For a directory of engine and threshing shows, Stemgas Publishing Company issues an annual directory. Contact Stemgas at: P.O. Box 328, Lancaster, PA 17603, 717-392-0733

The cost of the directory has been $5. It lists shows in virtually every area of the country. Stemgas also publishes *Gas Engines* magazine and *Iron-men Album*; magazines for the enthusiast.

Clubs and Newsletters

Newsletters that provide a wealth of information and lore about individual brands of antique farm tractors and equipment have been on the scene for some time. More spring up each year; the following list is far from complete.

Antique Power
P.O. Box 838
Yellow Springs, OH 45387

Ford/Fordson Collectors Association
645 Loveland-Miamiville Rd.
Loveland, OH 45140

Green Magazine
RR 1
Bee, NE 68314

I.H. Collectors
RR 2, Box 286
Winamac, IN 46996

M-M Corresponder (Minneapolis-Moline)
Rt. 1, Box 153,
Vail, IA 51465

9N-2N-8N Newsletter (Ford)
154 Blackwood Ln.
Stamford, CT 06903

Old Abe's News (Case)
Rt. 2, Box 2427
Vinton, OH 45686

Old Allis News (Allis Chalmers)
10925 Love Rd.
Belleview, MI 49021

Oliver Collector's News
Rt. 1
Manvel, ND 58256-0044

Prairie Gold Rush (Minneapolis-Moline)
Rt. 1
Walnut, IL 61376

Red Power (International Harvester)
Box 277
Battle Creek, IA 51006

Wild Harvest (Massey-Harris)
1010 S. Powell, Box 529
Denver, IA 50622

Restoration Specialists and Parts Suppliers

Brandon Pfieffer
7810 Upper Mt. Vernon Rd.
Mt. Vernon, IN 47620

K. Johnson
6530 Maple Grove Rd.
Cloquet, MN 55720

Antique Tractor Restoration
Huntley, IL

Wengers, Inc.
251 S. Race St.
Meyerstown, PA 17067

K & K Antique Tractors
RR 3 Box 384X
Shelbyville, IN 46176

Polacek Implement
Phillips, WI 54555
(Specializing in Ford and Allis Chalmers parts)

Steiner Tractor Parts, Inc.
G-10096 S. Saginaw
Holly, MI 48442
(New and used parts, write for catalog)

Machinery Hill
Phillips, WI 54555
(New and used parts)

Vernon Fossum
118 Freemont St.
Northfield, MN 55057
(Specializes in Ford governor rebuilding)

Minn-Kota
RR 1, Box 99
Milbank, SD 57252
(Specializes in steering wheel rebuilding)

Strojney Implement
Mosinee, WI 54455
(Ford and Ferguson parts and rebuilding)

Gap Tractor Salvage
Box 97
Cranfills Gap, TX 76637

Jimbo's Antique Tractor and Salvage
Rt. 2
Rock Island, TN 38581

Wilken and Sons Wrecking
Nashua, IA 50658
Palmer Fossum Fords
10201 E. 100th St.
Northfield, MN 55057
(Specializes in Fordson, Ford, and Ferguson parts
and restoration)

Fordson House
Escanaba, MI
(Specializes in Fordson Parts)

Ford Tractor Specialty
Marlo Remme
RR 1, Box 281
Dennison, MN 55018
(Specializes in Fordson, Ford through 800 Series,
and Fordson Major Diesel)

Rosewood Machine and Tool Co.
Duane Helman
Box 17
Rosewood, OH 43070
(Specializes in custom castings and Fordsons)

M. E. Brison
2731 Blacklick Eastern
Millersport, OH 43046
(Decal specialist)
Oliver Smith
305 S. 2nd St.
Denton, MD 21629
(Decal specialist)

Speer Cushion Company
431 S. Interocean
Holyoke, CO 80734
(Specializes in seat covers and cushions)

Griot's Garage
1228 Keystone Way
Vista, CA 92083
(Tools for tool junkies)

Emstrom Farm Antiques
RR 2, Box 140
Galesburg, IL 61401
Dwight Emstrom, Collector, Restorer, Parts, Sales
and Equipment

Index